TROUBLE WITH PARSNIPS

Laurel Decher

A Seven Kingdoms Fairy Tale

Copyright © 2018 Laurel Decher
All rights reserved. No part of this publication may be reproduced, stored in a retrieval system, or transmitted in any form or by any means electronic, mechanical, photocopying, recording, or otherwise without permission in writing from the publisher, except by reviewers, who may quote brief passages in a review. Thank you for respecting this author's hard work of this author.

ISBN 978-3-9820075-0-2 (Paperback Edition)
ISBN 978-3-9820075-1-9 (Hardcover Edition)
ISBN 978-3-9820075-2-6 (ebook Edition)

Library of Congress Control Number: 2018907982

Characters and events in this book are fictitious. Any similarity to real persons, living or dead, is coincidental and not intended by the author. Cochem Castle was inspired by rooks flying above the Reichsburg Cochem, not by dungeon workshops for inventors, croquet fever, or moats. The Pfalz (Burg Pfalzgrafenstein), on an island in the middle of the Rhine River, inspired the Blackfly Kingdom. Its dungeon is just as Nero describes, but no one plays croquet there. My wonderful Toastmasters International club in Burlington, Vermont sparked the Vintner's Ventriloquism League but all VVL speakers and speeches are fiction.

Printed and bound in the United States of America.

Published by Bumpity Boulevard Press.
P.O. Box 191
Peacham, VT, USA 05862
Visit https://LaurelDecher.com

Publisher's Cataloging-in-Publication data
Names: Decher, Laurel, author.
Title: Trouble with parsnips / Laurel Decher.
Series: A Seven Kingdoms Fairy Tale
Description: Peacham, VT: Bumpity Boulevard Press, 2018.
Identifiers: ISBN 978-3-9820075-1-9 (Hardcover) | 978-3-9820075-0-2 (pbk.) | 9783982007526 (ebook) | LCCN 2018907982
Summary: A nameless princess re-invents herself and saves her kingdom when she learns to speak up in a crisis.
Subjects: LCSH Kings, queens, rulers, etc.--Fiction. | Public speaking--Fiction. | Inventors--Fiction. | Inventions--Fiction. | Self-actualization (Psychology)--Fiction. | Fantasy. | BISAC JUVENILE FICTION / Fantasy & Magic | JUVENILE FICTION / Humorous Stories | Juvenile Fiction / Social Themes/ Self-Esteem & Self-Reliance
Classification: LCC PZ7.D3557 Tr 2018 | DDC [Fic]--dc23

CONTENTS

I.	A Delayed Party	1
II.	Too Late for Parsnips	13
III.	The Fairy Godmother Takes Her Time	26
IV.	Out of the Dishwater and Into the Storm	39
V.	A Rocky Situation	51
VI.	A Princely Rescue	61
VII.	Charming Complications	72
VIII.	Speaking Clearly with Tact Is an Art	82
IX.	The Rook Egg	95
X.	Brooding in the Dungeon	109
XI.	The Peppermint Tea House	124
XII.	Early for a Change	137
XIII.	Dungeon Hospitality	147
XIV.	The Second-Best Croquet Mallets	157
XV.	Speech or Die	165
XVI.	The Queen's Wager	176
XVII.	The Entry Basket	192
XVIII.	A Library Crisis	201
XIX.	The InterKingdom Tournament	215
XX.	The Pepper Pot Duel	224
XXI.	Making a Name	234
XXII.	Epilogue	248

For Jan, who makes my life shiny.

CHAPTER ONE
A Delayed Party

INSIDE COCHEM CASTLE, the nameless princess ducked underneath the head table to her self-appointed station. Her place of honor at the table was too far away. She'd waited ten years for this party and couldn't risk it going off the rails. Sitting on the rushes, with King Oliver's feet on one side and Queen Sibyl's on the other, the princess could hear everything.

Above her head, the shiny Golden Parsnip—the badge of his kingly power—hung from her father's belt.

The princess patted the hidden pocket of her gown. The drawing of her secret weapon, the Cloud of Defense, crinkled reassuringly. Along the back wall, the Cochem archers stood ready for King Oliver's command.

King Oliver "whispered" in Queen Sibyl's ear, and the princess smiled. Neither of her parents was any good at whispering. She made out the words with no trouble. King Oliver had to shout to be heard over the courtiers and guests.

"You're sure about which one needs a name?" King Oliver's best dancing shoes pivoted towards Queen Sibyl.

A Delayed Party

Wary of getting pinched, the princess kept an eye on the King's shoes and reminded herself that parents forgot things. Especially parents with fifteen children and a kingdom to govern. It wasn't personal. Besides, people without names were hard to remember.

Queen Sibyl stamped her small foot, and her silk skirts rustled. "Yes, of course. She's the one that put all those goldfish in the moat."

Mamma had noticed! Training five hundred brilliant-orange goldfish to spell out "NAME ME" had been worth it.

Confident that her parents were on board, the princess slipped under the dessert sluice to check a leaking seam. Keeping things dry was a full-time job with an artificial creek running through the hall. She didn't mind. As soon as she'd seen a diagram for a gold-panning sluice in a library book, she'd wanted to build one. Gold wasn't a big deal in Cochem, so they used it for dessert instead.

No one would notice if the guest of honor slipped away for a moment. Her parents had enough to do. The Kingdom's business took most of their attention, and educating the older Cochem children—the ones who might actually rule one day—took the rest. No one kept track of the youngest child in the family. A long time ago, the princess had decided to make the most of it. Sometimes, it made up for being called "Fifteenth."

"—a moment ago."

Even with the Seven Kingdoms partying it up, the end of Queen Sibyl's sentence carried down to the princess, whose head was now under the other end of the dessert sluice.

"She knows how to take care of herself," King Oliver's

voice rumbled on. "Handy around the castle too."

The princess, fishing a wrench out of her hall toolbox, wondered who they were talking about. King Oliver's sister, Queen Ash? "Handy" didn't seem right, but the Blackfly Queen definitely took care of herself. The princess frowned. Her favorite wrench for this job was in her workshop in Cochem's unused dungeon. She'd have to make do with this one.

"I thought the boy with the hair did the goldfish thing." King Oliver always made a swishing motion over his head to show the boy's pompadour hairstyle. "You know, Harold number three. But wait—goldfish are quite slippery for a baby, aren't they? Did the others do such things before they were christened?"

The princess didn't interrupt. She wanted to know what else they knew about her. Listening was always more useful than talking.

The king and queen tried to sort out their offspring. They got muddled after the seventh and came to a complete stop at number fourteen.

"Let's start again. We've got seven girls," King Oliver said.

Eight, thought the princess, but she tightened a bolt on the dessert sluice and gave her parents a moment more.

"And seven Harolds," Queen Sibyl said. "So she must be the fourteenth. But that doesn't seem right. Oh, how silly! The girl without a name is why we're here. So what number child does that make her?"

Speaking into the pipe, the nameless princess prompted, "The Fifteenth Child of our house."

King Oliver said, "What did you say?"

"I didn't say anything—" Queen Sibyl dropped her voice to

A Delayed Party

a confidential tone, no quieter than King Oliver's "—you see, the problem is, we forgot about christening this one. Things kept coming up, and now she's ten."

"Is that so?" King Oliver got to his feet, and the thump he gave the table made it tremble. He'd never called the hall to order for her before. The nameless princess smiled down at her christening gown. Queen Sibyl knew she was ten years old. This was going better than she'd hoped.

A tiny piece of paper on the rushes caught the princess's attention. She picked it up and read, "Twyla."

The other side was blank. She didn't know anyone called Twyla, but she pocketed the paper for her name collection. Writing "Fifteenth" at the top of school papers got old in a hurry.

"Rose, Marigold, Magenta, Saffron, Indigo . . ." King Oliver ran through the kingdoms present in the hall and sat down again. "The Blackflies aren't here." He exhaled in a way that made the princess worry he was finished. "Having the feast before the christening is a good idea. It should give them, maybe five extra hours. That should be enough, even for them, don't you think?"

At Sibyl number seven's christening, the Blackfly Kingdom was seven hours late. When the nameless princess heard that story, she adjusted the schedule for her own. She had a lot of practice adjusting things. Taking a better grip on her wrench, she tightened the next bolt.

"If we wait too long, the other guests will leave, and we still won't have a christening." Queen Sibyl coughed. "If Cook would at least send up the peppermint tea. My throat is a little dry. And you sound like you might be getting a cold. Are you feeling well enough for a bit of croquet after dinner?"

Croquet? The nameless princess froze, wrench in mid-air. It couldn't be croquet fever. This year, the whole family had gotten their shots.

"Now there's an idea." King Oliver's heel bounced on the rushes covering the hall's stone floor. "I'm always well enough for that. We could try the vineyard behind the castle. If the archers stand at the bottom of the rows, they can bowl the balls back up again. While I'm thinking about it, we're still missing black mallets and croquet balls. We have all the other kingdoms' colors."

Not today. The nameless princess set down her wrench and whipped through the crowd towards her royal parents. This couldn't happen. If the royal guests started knocking balls through wickets, they'd be scattered throughout the Seven Kingdoms before you knew it. It would be the end of the christening.

Her royal parents were losing focus. The princess dove back under the head table to keep tabs on things.

King Oliver called the steward over and ordered some mallets and balls painted black.

"Good idea! The Blackfly family got so annoyed last time when we didn't have their color." The hem of Queen Sibyl's dress went up and down in agreement. She was a vigorous nodder. The feather on top of her dozen-eggs hairstyle must be making a breeze. "Queen Ash is always so quick to feel slighted."

"It's their plague-y blackflies, you know. She can't stand'em." King Oliver always made excuses for his sister. "I mean—what if blackflies followed you everywhere you went?"

A Delayed Party

Queen Sibyl shuddered all the way down to her silvery hem. "Dreadful. I'd much rather talk about croquet. How about a quick game with the appetizers?"

Oh no. If only the Blackfly family would show up, blackflies and all. A royal christening couldn't start until all Seven Kingdoms had arrived.

The princess had to do something. But what?

At that moment, the headwaiter brought the banquet menu for final approval. Queen Sibyl wasn't wearing her glasses for the party, so King Oliver had to put on his reading glasses. Once they were on his nose, he winced. "With these darn things, I can't see past the end of my ... croquet mallet."

Considering one desperate plan after another, the princess made her way down the head table to the door. As she passed Harold number one, he bumped her fist with his. "Don't forget—if you run into your fairy godmother, be cool."

Sibyl number one called from the middle of the table, "Whatever you do, don't tell her what to give you."

"Yeah, just look at Queen Ash," Harold number three said in the princess's ear. "We don't need blackflies in Cochem."

"No matter what else you have to do, don't walk away." Sibyl number six had been caught by her fairy godmother on the way to the royal privy and knew what she was talking about.

Fourteen siblings meant you knew what to expect. The princess was glad she wasn't an only child, like the Blackfly Prince.

Reaching the hall door, she went out to the stables. The party could start if people thought the Blackfly Kingdom had arrived. She couldn't pretend to be Queen Ash or King Schwartz, so she'd have to pretend to be Prince Nero. He was about her age. She'd put on black clothes, and no one would know the difference. By now, the guests were too hungry to ask questions.

Once all Seven Kingdoms were present—or appeared to be present—food would be served, and everyone would be happy. The princess couldn't risk an impromptu croquet tournament. Even if this wasn't the fever.

She wasn't much bigger than Harold number seven, the brother closest in age to the princess. No Blackfly horses had arrived in the stables, so the princess tucked up her brocade skirt, put on an old pair of Harold number seven's black riding pants, and blacked her white Icelandic pony, Númi, with a pot of shoe-polish.

Wrapping herself in black saddle blankets, she tied a black knitted scarf over her light brown hair. She tiptoed barefoot up the spiral stairs to the gallery over the hall, to see if she really had to go through with this.

The silver Cochem banners on the walls gleamed in the torchlight. At her family's table on the dais, the princess's fourteen siblings played table hockey with the salt cellar. King Oliver had pushed his chair back as if the feast were over. His reading glasses still rested on his nose. Queen Sibyl swept up salt from the silver-linen tablecloth with her tiny, silver-handled brush and dustpan.

On the main floor of the hall, the seven remaining tables were arranged around the hearth fire like the slanted spokes of a wheel. The christening guests wore the showy colors of their kingdoms so that the hall looked like a silver-striped lollipop. Raspberry-scented Roses, perfumed

A Delayed Party

Daffodils, spicy Marigolds, fluffy Fuchsia, Siberian Iris, and rare black Tulips made a gorgeous, fragrant pinwheel.

Only the dimly lit black Tulips table had no guests. The Blackfly royal family still hadn't arrived. The princess straightened. If she wanted a name, it was time for action.

On the way down to the hall and the door out to the stables, she tried a new name aloud at each step:

Twyla.

   Cecily.

      Sylvia.

         Yolanda.

            Calypso.

               Amberly.

                  Gwendolyn.

Anything but Sibyl.

All seven of her sisters were named Sibyl. She'd never stand out in that crowd.

A few moments later, she whispered to the royal steward at the door so he'd announce her properly. A Blackfly banner would have helped. Then she mounted Númi, rode through the open portcullis into the feasting hall, and made her pony paw his hooves in the air.

To the assembled crowd, the royal steward roared, "Prince Nero of the Blackfly Kingdom pays his respects to the youngest princess of Cochem."

The Marigold Kingdom guests clapped their hands onto their ears and shook their heads, frowning. They were jumpy about loud voices.

"Good boy," the princess added under her breath to Númi. That book about the Spanish Riding School had been worth it. She dismounted, tossed the reins to a waiting

TROUBLE WITH PARSNIPS

stableboy, and accepted a swig of peppermint tea.

The guests from the Magenta Kingdom murmured to each other. "Finally. Now we can eat."

The Saffron Kingdom crown princess looked up from the saffron booties she was knitting. "Funny. Not as many blackflies as usual. Did they drain their swamp?"

Worrying about the lack of a Blackfly banner, the princess had forgotten about the blackflies. She flashed a disdainful look at the Saffron Kingdom table—as if she really were a Blackfly royal—and held her breath.

At the head table, her parents rose.

"They sent him all alone," murmured Queen Sibyl, squinting. "How did he ever find us? I heard he has a terrible sense of direction, poor thing."

"Welcome, Prince Nero!" King Oliver smoothed his thick mustache and beard in a considering way. He took off his reading glasses, and his eyes rested her face.

Uh, oh. She'd been sure he would forget about his reading glasses. He'd recognize her, and the christening would come to an unpleasant end.

But King Oliver unbuckled the Golden Parsnip, held it up high, and called out, "The Seven Kingdoms are here! Let the festivities begin!"

Suddenly dizzy, the princess gripped the nearest table edge. He hadn't recognized her. Why did she feel so hollow?

She should be happy. He wasn't supposed to tell the difference between the Blackfly prince and his own daughter. It would have ruined everything. She put up a proud chin, forced a brittle smile and strode off towards the black Tulips.

Queen Sibyl announced the program for the day. "We

A Delayed Party

hope you'll enjoy the feast. There are seventeen courses, one for each member of the royal family." The hall exploded into applause, and the queen smiled shyly. She was the only other one in the family who didn't care for speeches. "Afterwards, there will be the christening—"

The princess was relieved to hear it.

"Then we'll have jousting, footraces, and that game with the spinning tops. I can never remember what it's called—" she looked at King Oliver.

His whisper carried throughout the hall, "Carom, it's called carom."

"Thank you, dear. You all know what it's called, so there's only one more thing to say." Queen Sibyl spread out her arms. "Let the feast begin!"

The squeak of door hinges made everyone laugh. King Oliver never oiled the hinges for the doors that led to the royal kitchens. He said he wanted to prevent sneak attacks by his fifteen children, but the princess knew better. The sound was an appetizer for the feast.

Squeak, squeak. Squeak, squeak.

A long line of kitchen staff bore trays and trays of marvelous-smelling parsnip fries into the hall. The princess took advantage of the moment to slip under the black Tulips table. Sheltered by the table linen, she unwound herself from the black saddle blankets, wriggled out of Harold number seven's old riding pants, and took the black knitted scarf off her head. Her brocade skirt was a little crushed, but she was going to get a name.

The princess went the long way around and took her place at the bottom of the head table. She crunched a parsnip fry between her teeth and grinned at her seven sisters, dressed in matching brocade gowns, all talking at top speed.

The four oldest were comparing the fine points of all the Seven Kingdoms' princes and the three youngest the fine points of desserts to come. Nobody had missed her.

Her favorite course was the first. The parsnips were the perfect reddish-brownish-goldish color and tasted a little sweet and a little salty.

She couldn't enjoy the other courses properly. Now that she'd gotten away with impersonating the Blackfly prince, she was having second thoughts. What would happen when the real Blackfly prince arrived?

Even though she knew the kitchen doors were the only squeaky ones, she checked the hall entrance every time.

The Blackfly family didn't show up for the field lettuce salad with toasted walnuts, the crispy potato pancakes with applesauce, the green asparagus with toasted pine nuts and a sprinkling of salt, the fresh spinach salad with strawberries, the buttermilk soup with snippets of chives, or the artichokes you ate by dipping each tiny leaf in lemony-garlic sauce and nibbling off the tender inner edge.

They missed the crispy fried fish, the radish roses in all colors, the potato croquettes with ketchup, the tiny cooking pans for melting Swiss cheese, the cauliflower "trees" with hot, buttered breadcrumbs, the thinly sliced lean roast pork with dumplings and gravy, the baby peas in the pod with tureens to cook them, and the fruit platters glowing with rubies that were really pomegranate seeds.

They didn't even show up for the tiny cheese wheels covered in red wax.

The feast's sparkling finale was the princess's second

A Delayed Party

favorite course. Water wheels and jets propelled miniature boats along sluices all around the hall. Each boat carried one serving of dessert. No one ever remembered she'd made the dessert sluice, but everyone enjoyed it.

When a guest pointed to a cake, pie, torte, or tart they liked, a footman fished out the little boat, blotted off the bottom, and gave it to the guest with a bow. The princess, and her fourteen brothers and sisters, preferred helping themselves.

She had just plucked a kayak with a chocolate cream puff out of the gurgling stream when King Oliver said, "Prince Nero's not old enough to sign the christening certificate, is he?"

"He was born about the same time as Harold number seven." Queen Sibyl counted on her fingers. "That makes him eleven, so no, he's not. Do you think Ash isn't coming then?"

The princess froze. She knew all Seven Kingdoms had to be present for the christening, but she hadn't realized they had to sign off. The kayak dropped from her hand back into the sluice, making waves that shipwrecked a dozen cakes. Her fourteen royal brothers and sisters protested, but she paid no attention.

Her boat floated down the sluice, out of reach.

CRAAACK!

The princess spun around. The front doors of the banquet hall banged open, revealing the portcullis, smashed in two. *Oops.* She should have told the stableboy to leave it open. A cloud of blackflies blew in.

CHAPTER TWO
Too Late for Parsnips

THE BLACKFLY RULERS, King Schwartz and the frowning Queen Ash, swept into the hall. The real Crown Prince Nero followed. Their black-clad archers brought up the rear in two long, scowling lines, carrying all their Blackfly Kingdom banners. As if Queen Ash wanted to make sure everyone knew who she was.

The princess glanced uneasily at her parents. Prince Nero looked taller than Harold number seven.

"Oh dear," King Oliver said, under his breath.

It was her christening. Time to step up. She wished her gown was a little less crumpled and hoped some special treatment would sweeten Queen Ash's temper. The princess got a footman to fill two welcome cups—one with fresh grape juice and one with fresh peppermint tea because you never knew what people liked—and carried them to the newcomers.

And stood there without words until her arms shook.

Queen Ash made no move to take a cup. King Schwartz was looking at the dessert sluice with an expression of longing. Prince Nero stood a little behind them, at

Too Late for Parsnips

attention. The princess stood up a little straighter and became uncomfortably aware of a voice just beyond her elbow, at the Siberian Iris table.

"First, he rode in here on his pony, and now he's brought his parents. Did he lose them on the way?" The Indigo prince took a noisy slurp.

Next to him, an Indigo princess said, "This prince looks shorter. Maybe he's the younger brother."

The princess's smile hardened. If she didn't think of something to say, the Indigo Kingdom was going to figure out what she'd done. Unfortunately, she wasn't good at things to say. No surprise—fourteen older siblings covered it the rest of the time.

The noisy slurper said, "No, no. There's only one Blackfly prince. The pony made him look taller. And the thing-a-ma-bob on his head."

Prince Nero looked like he was trying not to smile, and a tiny wrinkle formed between his black eyebrows. The princess's face got warm. If she said something, maybe the Indigo Kingdom would stop speculating. She cleared her throat.

"Uh." She waggled the welcome cups. "Welcome."

Queen Ash's gaze was fixed on a point somewhere above the princess's head. King Schwartz had sidled towards the desert sluice. Without breaking protocol, Prince Nero stepped to the side of his parents and bowed his head as if she were more than the nameless fifteenth royal child of Cochem. He looked her in the eye. "Your Highness. Best wishes on your christening day."

He was good at formal stuff. The princess curtsied.

Queen Ash glowered but relented enough to take a cup.

TROUBLE WITH PARSNIPS

King Schwartz took one too. They both drank deep, and the whole hall held its breath, ready to cheer.

"Ow!" Queen Ash slapped at a black spot on her neck. Her fingers left a red splotch.

In spite of herself, the princess was interested. It was true then—a fairy godmother gift could bite you. The princess wondered if the queen had ever tried bug spray.

Queen Ash stomped over to King Oliver and Queen Sibyl, picked up an empty parsnip platter from the head table, and shook it. Salt flew over the tablecloth. "You ate the feast without us—"

"Well now, Prince Nero came hours ago. How were we to know you were still coming?" King Oliver tugged at his beard.

Oh no. Hoping to change the subject, the princess dashed around the hall with an empty platter, rounding up leftover parsnip fries from every table. She brought the sorry little heap to Prince Nero, standing by the head table. "Sorry."

His mouth quirked, but he took the platter.

"That's outrageous!" Queen Ash took a slightly burnt parsnip fry from Prince Nero and held it up.

"I don't know why we bother." Queen Ash gave King Oliver a withering look. "I wait months to taste the food of my childhood, but when we finally get here, the portcullis is closed in our faces, and you've already eaten. Well, now you're getting what's coming to you: We challenge you to the Duel of the Halls!"

Sibyl number seven said, "Not again—we always lose."

The princess groaned. *Double-whammy.* The Duel was only half of the package. It tested the Seven Kingdoms' defense.

Too Late for Parsnips

The InterKingdom Speech Tournament was the other half. It tested the Seven Kingdoms' young people.

Harold number three closed his eyes and fell forward in defeat. His forehead hit the head table with a clunk. He got it.

"It doesn't matter about the Duel." Sibyl number one sat up taller in her chair. "This time we'll finally have a chance at the Speech Tournament."

Sibyl number two smiled and nodded. They were the two best speakers in the family.

Needless to say, the nameless princess wasn't. Speakers without names were impossible to introduce, and it got worse from there. She stuck to tinkering with hot air balloons and cable ferries.

The sick feeling in her stomach got worse. Unless Cochem scored a quick win, a contest where one kingdom tried to skewer the other kingdom's banners with arrows meant the end of her christening party.

The Cochem banners were mounted on the stone walls all around the hall which meant arrows flying high in the air, in every direction. The Blackfly banners, in the princess's experience, could be anywhere at all, depending on where their queen put the archers who held them. Queen Ash had a flexible view of rules.

Arms outstretched, Queen Ash swept a circle all the way around the hall. Blackflies swarmed out of her long black sleeves. Her fairy godmother gift was nasty.

Royal guests shouted and swatted.

"Gotcha!"

"Eeeek!"

"I hate these things!"

"Hold still—" King Oliver swatted a blackfly on Queen Sibyl's arm, apologized for the swat, and straightened to address the hall. "I'd much rather play a game or two of croquet."

"Couldn't we eat something first?" The Blackfly King Schwartz took one look at his queen's rigid face and sighed. "Queen Ash doesn't care for croquet—"

"I said the Duel of the Halls." Queen Ash waved her arms in a wild swatting motion, knocking over the huge bouquet of Siberian Iris and spilling water into the laps of the Indigo Kingdom royal family.

More blackflies poured out of her sleeves. Various Indigo princes and princesses jumped up and mopped with their napkins. It was like a dance.

Swat. Blot. Swat. Wipe. Swat.

King Oliver sighed. "Very well, if you insist."

The nameless princess grabbed a bale of napkins from the nearest footman and took them to the far end of the Indigo table. She blinked her blurry eyes so she wouldn't trip.

She hiccupped—the kind that hurt—and pressed it with her hand. A Tournament would distract her royal parents for months.

Pointlessly. Prince Nero was the only young person in the Blackfly Kingdom, but he always won the Speech Tournament. Queen Ash saw to that.

Basically, Cochem had to win the Duel to keep the Tournament from happening. But how? Would the princess's secret weapon be enough?

"Where are my archers?" King Oliver called out.

The Cochem archers filed into the hall and presented

their bows. "Here, sire."

"The Kingdom of Cochem accepts your challenge! Who will referee?" King Oliver's gaze swept the hall, and the princess had a moment of hope.

If no referee could be found, the Duel could be postponed.

But the guests at the Magenta Kingdom table immediately waved their arms.

"We accept the Magenta Kingdom as referee," Queen Ash said.

"Thank you, King Pink." King Oliver acknowledged the referee with a bow. The princess wished the Magenta Kingdom was a little less helpful.

The Magenta Kingdom guests clattered up the spiral stair to the gallery overlooking the hall. The princess didn't blame them. The latticework kept most of the stray arrows out. Harold number three had told her the Magenta Kingdom wasn't known for bravery under fire.

"Ready!" King Pink called.

"Draw!" Queen Ash commanded.

Twenty-four Blackfly archers drew, aiming at Cochem banners on every wall in the hall.

"Fire at will!"

The archers loosed their arrows. Their bowstrings twanged like the strings of a badly tuned harp. Arrows filled the air.

The Saffron Kingdom party dove under their table as one. Daffodils waved back and forth in their vases like anxious ducks. Quivering bouquets on the remaining tables showed that the other kingdoms had followed Saffron's lead.

Most arrows skittered harmlessly from the stone walls,

but one skewered a Cochem banner over the princess's head. She took refuge behind the dessert fountain. An arrow struck the Marigold Kingdom's bouquet, and spicy orange petals exploded into the air.

A low arrow skimmed the sluice beside the princess, and lodged itself in a chocolate cream puff. The princess was pierced with a pang. A Duel of the Halls on her christening day!

From the gallery, King Pink counted aloud. "One, Two, Three for the Blackfly Kingdom."

That was terrible. Three Cochem banners already skewered and only four untouched. If the Blackflys kept it up, they'd win in the very next round. A victory for Queen Ash meant millions of blackflies, fleeing guests, and a deserted Cochem.

Cochem's excellent archers were next. The princess went still: hitting the target wasn't the problem. Queen Ash's rule-bending was.

Faint clapping came from the Saffron Kingdom, back under the table.

Taking advantage of the lull, King Schwartz fished out the cream puff by its arrow and licked chocolate cream off his fingers.

The Blackfly archers lowered their banners and formed a tight circle. The princess's eyebrows went up. A circle was cheating. Banners were supposed to be mounted in the wall brackets or, worst case, held up in a straight line, well above the archers' heads. If an arrow struck an archer instead of a banner, your kingdom was disqualified.

But King Oliver never shot at archers in a Duel, and Queen Ash knew it.

Too Late for Parsnips

Queen Ash tapped her foot. "Kingdom of Cochem—Do you yield?"

The princess had to remind King Oliver about their secret weapon. The Cloud of Defense could capture banners without hitting anyone. She yanked her drawing out of her pocket, folded it into a paper airplane, aimed at King Oliver, and let fly.

Tink!

The tiny airplane struck the ceremonial ribbons on King Oliver's chest and fell onto the head table.

"What's this?" The King brushed off his ribbons and picked up the paper.

From the other side of the hall, the princess willed him to open it. It was so hard to get people to understand what you meant. A drawing was better, but people actually had to look at it.

He unfolded the airplane and studied the paper. Borrowing Queen Sibyl's magnifying glass, he adjusted it and moved the paper back and forth a few times. Finally, he stopped. His eyebrows knit together, and his mouth pursed.

Would he try it?

"Yield?" King Oliver focused the magnifying glass towards Queen Ash. His eye was giant behind the lens. "In our own hall?" He turned to his archers and made a jabbing motion at the ceiling.

The signal.

He'd remembered. The princess's heart skipped a beat. Maybe there was still hope for the christening.

The head archer shot his silver arrow straight up into the air. A fine cord trailing from the arrow was attached to the center of a round silver parachute emblazoned with the

Cochem standard. The Cloud of Defense.

Thunk.

Directly above the Blackfly archers, the arrowhead bit into the ceiling beam. The feathered shaft quivered, but the arrow held.

A split second later, the other Cochem archers loosed their arrows, all attached by shorter cords to the parachute's edge.

The princess held her breath. Would it work properly inside the crowded hall?

Launched into the air, the silk billowed and filled. The Cloud hovered for a millisecond and sank down over the horrified Blackfly archers, neatly covering all their black banners with Cochem's huge silver one. Not a scrap of black showed.

Thud, snap, thud, thud, thud, snap, thud, thud, snap, thud.

The arrows pinned the shorter cords to the earthen floor.

The princess jumped up and down, clapping. All seven Blackfly banners at once! Queen Ash had to sit down and behave herself now. The christening was on.

Harold number three made a megaphone out of his hands. "And Cochem bags the win!"

"Cochem! Cochem! Cochem!" The other Harolds and the Sibyls chanted and clapped until the hall rang with sound. Cochem had never won a Duel of the Hall before.

The Saffron Kingdom came out from under their table and joined in.

Queen Ash had already lost, but she was still shouting commands. "If that old trick beats you, you should be ashamed of yourselves. Lean over! Dump that silly thing off your heads!"

Her archers writhed with their heavy banners under the silk parachute, but some leaned to one side, and some leaned to another. The archers managed to slip out from underneath the Cloud. But when they tried to get their banners out, they tripped over each other and fell onto the rushes.

Four Blackfly banners fell into the glowing hearth and burst into flames.

Uh, oh. The princess had to get to the emergency sluice levers. They were built into the wall next to the empty Magenta Kingdom table. The only way through the commotion was . . . underneath! Ducking under tables and sprinting in between, she crossed the hall: Rose, Saffron—still crowded under there—Marigold, and Magenta Kingdoms.

"One-Two-Three-Four for Cochem!" shouted King Pink from behind the latticework.

Cochem had won the first match. But unless they got this fire out, they'd have to forfeit to save the castle. The princess yanked on the lever that drained the dessert sluices of water.

Uh! It was stuck. The heat must have warped it out of shape.

Ouch. Swat. Ouch.

Now that she was standing still, the blackflies bit her hands again and again. Honestly. Who needed fairy godmother gifts like these? Her own fairy godmother hadn't shown up. The princess hoped she never would. A name would be enough, thank you.

On the other side of the hall, the frantic Blackfly archers yanked on the snarled poles and banners, puffing up the

TROUBLE WITH PARSNIPS

Cloud of Defense, which fanned the hearth like giant bellows.

Whoosh, Whoosh . . . Poof!

The rushes nearest the hearth caught fire, and smoke plumed in every direction. There was no time to lose. Coughing, the princess wiggled the emergency sluice lever gently back and forth. Something was blocking the lever.

"Let fly!" Queen Ash commanded her archers, even though thick smoke filled the hall.

Always a thoughtful host, King Oliver bawled, "Cochem forfeits! Eeeeeeeee-verybody out!"

Guests, hosts, archers, and referees fled, still swatting blackflies. With her pocketknife, the princess pried a tiny piece of rush out of the mechanism. She pulled the lever.

Water doused the burning rushes and boiled on the hot stones with a loud *zissssch*.

Steam filled the hall.

The Black Tulip table settings were untouched. The perfectly folded napkins waited for her christening to begin. Choking, the still nameless princess made her way out. She couldn't blame King Oliver. A good King protected his guests. If he hadn't forfeited the Duel, Queen Ash would have skewered them all.

But the Speech Tournament was going to make a name impossible. The princess sagged in the doorframe.

Nothing had gone the way she'd hoped, but it hadn't all been for nothing. Had it?

She told herself it could have been worse. The royal family could have come down with croquet fever. The Tournament could have required every royal child to give a speech. She shuddered. A fate worse than death.

Too Late for Parsnips

Squaring her shoulders, she went out to survey the damage. If she wanted to feel any better, she needed to do some work with her hands.

※ ※ ※

With a loud roar, the roof over one of the Tower windows burst into flame, lighting up the night sky. The princess ran down below the castle to join the royal firefighters at the pump.

The fire had gotten so big so fast. Hadn't her emergency sluice worked at all?

Shale from the roof exploded into a hundred fragments. The princess covered her head with her arms and ran for shelter. Royal firefighters leaped out of the way of falling timber.

"Back!" The Fire Chief ordered. "Get that pump going!"

Then, the roof fell in. Smoke poured out of the windows like a never ending line of ghosts leaving the royal portrait gallery.

For fifteen terrible long minutes, no water came out of the hoses. The princess must have gotten something wrong. Firefighters blocked her from the pump, so she went over the design in her mind, searching for a mistake. It all checked.

Then she followed the hoses along the ground. A big stone block from the castle had fallen onto the hoses and pinched them shut. She yanked the block, but it was too heavy to move. If she could lift this end up even a tiny bit, the force of the water might straighten the hoses all by itself.

The other firefighters had thrown the useless hoses to one side and were chopping away at a burning section of the castle, too busy to stop and help, even if she could tell them what she needed.

Heat from the fire burned her hands and face. She had to hurry. Taking a crowbar from a massive firefighter's toolbox, she eased it under the edge of the block and pushed down on the crowbar with all her weight.

The block came up a tiny bit, and water pushed in the hoses under the block, taking some pressure off the crowbar. She threw herself down on the crowbar, and the block came up a little more, letting more water in the hose.

The water pushed up against the block which tilted and crashed on its side, settling with a thud and freeing the hoses. They filled and fattened like snakes and water gushed out of the nozzles, spraying the firefighters.

"Hey!" The firefighter wiped the water off his face in one quick motion, picked up the hoses, and got to work on the splintered wood.

Hoorah! The princess did a cartwheel right there on the grass.

For several hours afterwards, the firefighters pumped water from the river and sprayed the steaming stone walls of the castle. The princess ran around everywhere, helping wherever she saw something to do.

It was well after midnight before the fire was out, and everyone could go to sleep.

CHAPTER THREE

The Fairy Godmother Takes Her Time

WHEN THE PRINCESS woke the next morning, she was alone in her dungeon workshop. It was hard to tell time because no light came in from outside, but she must have overslept. Fourteen cast-off sleeping bags littered the floor. Her brothers and sisters were already gone. She got up, stretched out the kinks from sleeping on the workbench, and hurried out of the dungeon, up the spiral stairs, and into the vineyards.

Drawing in big gulps of well-washed air, she followed the road out the castle gate. It was already the middle of the morning. Wind whipped her christening gown, smudged a bit from last night's firefighting.

Pennants waved above the colorful tents in the royal campground. The Seven Kingdoms were all still here. With an out-of-doors christening, the princess could still get a name. A robin burst into song. The princess sang right along with it.

Tying her hair to keep it out of her eyes, she took out her pocket spyglass and hunted for any sign of her family.

There! Next to the five rows of uprooted grapevines. That clump of black must be the Blackfly family creeping down towards a larger clump, of silver. Her own family. The princess ran straight down the steep aisle between the nearest two rows of grapevines and skidded to a stop, bumping King Oliver and grabbing Queen Sibyl by the sleeve to stop her fall.

"Ho, there!" King Oliver said, catching her.

The princess jumped on the moment. "Papa, the christening. Can we, *uh*, can we have it now?"

King Oliver blinked. "Right. Christening. Sibbie, do you see the Bishop anywhere?"

The princess froze.

"The Bishop?" Queen Sibyl had a fresh feather in her hat. She covered her mouth with her hand. "Oh dear! I'm not sure we invited him."

This couldn't be happening. This was just a nightmare brought on by too much smoke. The princess pinched herself.

Ouch. She'd been so sure the Blackfly family was the final required ingredient. None of her fourteen royal brothers and sisters had mentioned the Bishop. They'd been too busy telling her horror stories about fairy godmothers.

She studied King Oliver's face, hoping there was some way around the Bishop.

But King Oliver let go of her hand and sat down on a stone wall. Passing a shaky hand over his forehead, he asked, "Sibbie, when you close your eyes, do you see croquet wickets?"

Uh oh.

Queen Sibyl patted King Oliver's hand, but the next

The Fairy Godmother Takes Her Time

moment she was supporting herself with both hands on the stone wall. Gingerly, she sat down next to him. "But we got shots." It was almost a wail.

Croquet fever. The princess swallowed hard.

White and sweaty, Harold number one dashed up with an arm draped in wickets, like a cross between a medieval knight and a waiter. "Where should we set up the course?"

Every one of her brothers and sisters had a glazed look. Most held croquet equipment. Mallets swayed back and forth, croquet balls clonked together, metal wickets chimed, and it all added up to a croquet orchestra with 16 players.

An epidemic.

The more croquet they played, the faster they'd all recover, but the christening was done for. It could be two weeks before they were themselves again, and the Seven Kingdoms' guests would be long gone.

Huh. So far, the princess didn't feel the least urge to pick up a mallet. Her shot seemed to be working. But then, the Royal Physician had opened a new, 16-dose vial of vaccine just for her. When he had complained about the waste, the princess had suggested he use up the rest on the members of the castle staff. She hoped he had. With almost the whole royal family down with fever, a few vaccinated people would be a great help.

At that moment, the Blackfly family reached the terrace. Queen Ash went over to King Oliver and pushed his head back with a long, bony finger. "I'd say you were Unfit."

Noooo. The princess knew what Queen Ash was thinking. If King Oliver's family was Unfit, they needed a regent to rule until they were better.

TROUBLE WITH PARSNIPS

The princess opened her mouth to object, but Queen Ash beat her to it. "Give ME the Golden Parsnip, Oliver. I'll take care of everything until you're better."

Uh. Queen Ash—in perfect health—was ten times more Unfit than King Oliver with croquet fever. She'd only been in Cochem for one day, and look at the castle! The princess imagined blackfly-maddened players tripping over wickets, the Royal Physician wrapping various arms and legs in plaster, and Queen Ash whacking balls of every color off to distant Coventry. Cackling. While the Cochem Kingdom went to rack and ruin.

By now, Queen Sibyl was tracing imaginary croquet courses with her silver fork all over her silver linen napkin in desperate haste. With an admirable force of will, she stabbed her fork into the napkin to hold it still long enough to gasp out to King Oliver, "Let. Her. Plan. The. Tournament."

The princess smacked her own forehead. Not croquet—speeches. She'd been thinking about the christening, the Duel, the castle fire, and croquet fever, and forgotten all about the Tournament.

King Oliver's free hand hovered over the wickets on Harold number one's arm, but, at Queen Sibyl's words, he yanked his hand back. "But Sibbie, you always told me—"

The princess knew what King Oliver was about to say: Queen Ash should never rule the Cochem Kingdom. That was true. But his inability to whisper was about to cause another InterKingdom incident. Gripped by fever and madly tracing, Queen Sibyl couldn't stop him.

The princess's siblings and the Blackfly Crown Prince were knocking croquet balls up and down the rows of vines.

The Fairy Godmother Takes Her Time

King Schwartz was evidently keeping score.

This called for desperate measures. The princess stomped on King Oliver's toes.

"*Yeowp!*" King Oliver's fingers gripped the wickets on Harold number one's arm.

Queen Ash snickered.

King Oliver's eyes watered and the princess felt terrible. His eyebrows made a threatening hedge over his eyes, but then he seemed to catch himself. "Sibbie?" he said.

Still feverishly scribbling, Queen Sibyl gave a tiny shake of her head and closed her eyes. "I can't. I mean, look at me." She waved her fork and napkin.

His mouth drooped, but he nodded. "This should make you feel better." He gave her a handful of Harold's wickets.

The princess didn't have the least desire to grab one for herself. Proof that her shot must be working.

"Hand over the Golden Parsnip before chaos breaks out," Queen Ash snapped, stepping in front of the princess, who was wondering what Queen Ash's version of chaos was. "Your whole family is Unfit."

The princess had a soft voice, but she wasn't Unfit. Her hand shot up, waving back and forth.

Queen Ash took a step closer to King Oliver. "Come ON, Oliver. You never let me do anything BIG."

The princess jumped up on the stone wall and waved her hand above Queen Ash's shoulder. *Take me instead.* Calling out to King Oliver wouldn't work unless he was looking straight at her.

Tossing a croquet ball helplessly in the air and catching it, King Oliver didn't or couldn't look up. After all, the princess wasn't that tall, even on top of a wall.

TROUBLE WITH PARSNIPS

With his free hand, King Oliver unclasped the Golden Parsnip from his belt and held it out to Queen Ash. He rasped out, "Will you rule Cochem Fair and True?"

"Wait!" the princess said, but, as usual, her voice didn't carry. King Oliver didn't react. She bounced up and down on tip-toes, arm still in the air. She hadn't been brought up to rule a kingdom, but anything was better than handing Cochem over to the Blackflys.

"Of course," Queen Ash cooed to her brother and crossed her fingers behind her back.

The princess pointed at Queen Ash's crossed fingers and bawled out, "Hey!"

At least she felt like she'd bawled it out, but Queen Ash shushed her without looking, and no one else reacted. The fever had them all in a daze.

"Take the 15th." King Oliver mopped his brow with his silver handkerchief. "We should be well by then."

The princess wanted to ask for a later date. The fever would make her parents forget about her name, and the InterKingdom Speech Tournament would finish off the job. Seven Kingdoms' worth of people giving speeches meant a lot of tired listeners.

Then she had a terrible thought. What if she were the only one of her siblings healthy enough to give a speech at the Tournament? *Ew.* No one could make her give a speech, could they? Of course, Hugh would try. Just thinking about how that conversation would go made the princess queasy. King Oliver should make the Tournament a week later, just in case.

But when she looked up, King Oliver was shaking and pale. It wasn't the time to ask for personal favors. Her christening would have to wait a little longer. That was just how it was.

Two or three more years without her own library card. Life stretched out like a desert. No books.

She swallowed her disappointment.

"Next year, get your shot, Oliver." Queen Ash kissed the Golden Parsnip and hung it on the chain she always wore around her neck. She dismissed the Cochem family with a wave and a mocking laugh. "Let's find you a nice, out-of-the-way place to play—"

The princess wanted to know what the problem was with the shots, but Queen Ash was right about the fever playing itself out. There was no cure.

"Oooooh. I know the perfect place to keep you out of the way until I'm finished here." Shading her eyes, Queen Ash watched as her husband knocked King Oliver's ball into the Mosel River. "Well done, Schwartz!"

To King Oliver, she added, "On second thought, I'll take you myself. Just to be sure you . . . arrive. It's the perfect place to . . . recover."

The princess didn't like the sound of that. Queen Ash probably wanted solitude to toast giant marshmallows over Cochem's burning castle.

Queen Ash snatched a croquet ball and mallet, dropped the ball on the uneven ground of the vineyard and whacked it in the direction of the Blackfly Kingdom. "Your turn."

Queen Ash's "perfect place" must be her castle, the one on a rock in the middle of the Rhine River.

"Thank you, Ash. This fever is a little disorienting." King Oliver helped the shivering Queen Sibyl to her feet, and they swayed and chimed towards the croquet game already in progress.

"Fore!" King Oliver shouted and whacked a croquet ball. The silver ball flew up into the sky, made a graceful arc over the grapevines, and dropped into the middle of the game.

"Papa?" the princess called out, "Mamma?"

But they disappeared behind the hill. The princess longed to follow them, but until the fever played out, she was the only one who wasn't Unfit. She had a duty to Cochem.

Reluctantly, she turned away and headed back up to the sodden castle. Cochem needed defenses or they'd all be homeless later. Who knew what Queen Ash would try when she came back with the Golden Parsnip?

Something tickled the back of the princess's hand, and she tried to brush it off.

"Careful there!"

A voice? The princess stopped short. Who was still here? She spun around to see who hadn't followed the croquet game.

No one.

Something tickled her hand again, and she heard a distinct chuckle. She looked down at her hand.

A laughing damselfly?

She brought her hand up to eye-level. A tiny person with damselfly wings and flowing black, micro-braids stood on the princess's hand.

Smoke must make you see things. The princess blinked, rubbed her eyes with the other hand and looked again.

Miniature elephants marched around the hem of the creature's long tie-dye dress. The princess had always thought fairy godmothers would look more . . . dangerous.

"Don't tell me—I went right outta your head." The fairy

The Fairy Godmother Takes Her Time

reached out a tiny hand and pretended to pull something out of the princess's head. Her voice was surprisingly low and sweet for such a small creature. Not shrill at all. But she was frowning quite ferociously.

The princess struggled to come up with a diplomatic way of saying the party was already over, and the christening hadn't happened.

"Hello?" The fairy nudged the princess's hand with a tiny red sneaker.

"*Uh.* Can I set you down somewhere?" The princess looked around for an appropriate spot. "I have to go."

"Can you set me . . . can you *what!?*" The fairy put her hands on her hips. "You *do* know who I am?"

The princess's brothers and sisters had been very clear. Don't make magical godparents mad, or bad things happened to your whole family.

"Fairy godmother, ma'am, there was a castle fire last night." The princess stretched out her arm to make sure the fairy could see.

"No wonder there was such a racket. I thought you were shooting off the fireworks early." The fairy shook her braids and dusted her hands together. "It's a good thing I got here when I did. We'd better go around back. And you can call me Kizzy." She flew off, and the princess followed, feeling almost hopeful. If the fairy could magically defend the castle, the princess could set out after her family and bring them home to recover.

But in the shelter of Queen Sibyl's flower garden, Kizzy settled herself on a full-blown peony and propped her red sneakers up on its white petals, as if she had all the time in the world. "Let's give you your gift for governing the kingdom before it's too late."

Uh. Nothing with uncontrollable insects. Or rare fevers.

The princess had always thought you needed a name before you got a gift, but this wasn't the time for questions. With Queen Ash holding the Golden Parsnip, the princess needed all the help she could get. "That's very kind."

Kizzy took *Magical Gifts for Royal Christenings, Volume 1* out of her bag and opened it on her lap.

"Is it okay if I look over your shoulder?"

Kizzy's laugh was like gurgling water. "You're welcome to try."

The princess fished her spyglass out of her pocket, flipping it around to magnify the tiny letters inside the book. Kizzy gave her a nod of grudging approval.

"Can I cure croquet fever with magic?"

"Are you making fun of me?" Kizzy gave her a dirty look. "This isn't about superpowers."

"*Uh*. No." A superpower was what she needed, even if she wasn't supposed to ask for it. If she couldn't cure croquet fever, she'd take the power to defend the kingdom while Queen Ash relived her Cochem childhood, or the power to keep peace at the Speech Tournament.

She didn't know how to make Kizzy understand the situation. "*Uh*, I have to . . ." She pointed her index finger in the direction her family had taken and then jerked her thumb at the blackened castle, but Kizzy didn't take her eyes from the princess's face.

"Can't quite tell me, can you? Just what I suspected." Kizzy narrowed her eyes. "I've got the perfect gift for you."

The princess had a moment of pure fear. What if Kizzy gave her a gift even worse than Queen Ash's blackflies?

The Fairy Godmother Takes Her Time

Then her whole family would go from forgetting her to hating her.

If Cochem wasn't in crisis, the princess would ask for the power make her parents remember her long enough to give her a name. But that was wasteful. If she had a name, her family would remember about her without magic. Cochem was in a crisis, so this wasn't the time to think about herself.

She wanted to tell Kizzy to take her time, choose carefully, or don't do anything rash, but Kizzy had already run her finger down the index and found her entry while the princess was still deciding what to say.

"Here it is." Kizzy turned to a page in the main part of the book. "*Hiding in plain sight*. Let me look up the footnote."

Uh. This wasn't the time for footnotes. What was *hiding in plain sight* supposed to mean? If superpowers weren't available, how about the ability to calculate numbers without mistakes? Or the newest model of cable ferry. Then she could whisk her family home from the Blackfly Kingdom. Even a good book about how to build one would be welcome.

But you didn't tell fairy godmothers what to give you. So the princess stood there, mute, while her home was in shambles, and her feverish family wandered the Seven Kingdoms.

Kizzy leafed through endless pages of microscopic print. "Here—I have to read you this part, it's in the rules, so listen up: 'To lose this gift, you must persuade a person of a truth they don't want to hear.'"

Rules? There was no time for all of this.

Oblivious to the princess's distress, Kizzy said, "The

warnings section is much longer than usual, almost half a page."

The princess glanced down, and Kizzy pointed at yellow-highlighted lines that could have been ant footprints.

The princess's inverted spyglass was useless so she couldn't skip ahead. Ever since that unexpected explosion in her workshop, she read warning labels. "What does it say?"

Kizzy wiggled her sneakers. "Something spilled."

Normally, the princess would feel sympathetic. Accidents happened. Hugh Ancry—the ancient librarian of the Palace Agricultural Library—was the one who dressed people down for spills in books. But safety mattered. Warning labels needed to be readable. "You should be more careful."

Kizzy gave her a frosty look. "Life's not all about you godchildren, you know."

Since her godmother was ten years and a day too late, that wasn't exactly news. The princess tapped the page with a finger. "Could we, *uh*, get on with this . . . gift?"

"Very well." Kizzy shook out her dragonfly wings, raised her wand, and assumed a professional air. "This won't take a moment. Please stand a little closer."

A fine mist rained down the front of the littlest princess's christening gown. "Lovely, now turn around." The fine mist came again and tickled the back of the princess's neck.

"Enjoy! I have a few years before the next christening. Have to use my time wisely." Her fairy godmother plumped herself down on the peony and took out *Volume 2*. "Why don't you go tell some other people what you need?" She made an almost snorting noise, but her tiny handkerchief was over her face so fast, the princess couldn't tell.

The Fairy Godmother Takes Her Time

Since the day was half over, she didn't stop to find out.

After a curtsied good-bye-and-thank-you, she set out to conquer her To-Do List:

1. Get ready to defend the castle against Queen Ash and the Golden Parsnip.

2. Bring the Cochem family back as soon as one or more of them were healthy. (See number 1.)

3. Get a name before the InterKingdom Tournament made the princess's parents forget all about her again.

The last one wasn't royally important, like the first two, but it had to stay on her list. It wasn't on anyone else's.

CHAPTER FOUR

Out of the Dishwater and Into the Storm

By the time the princess left Queen Sibyl's flower garden, the morning's shadows were gone. Fairy godmother stuff took a while. She checked the trails in the distance for any signs of the returning Blackfly Queen. Nothing yet. But she'd be here soon enough. The princess took a shortcut through the ruined hall and came out the front of the castle.

The first rule of defending a castle was to prepare for a siege. Between Queen Ash's late entry to the feast and the entire Seven Kingdoms escaping in a rush after the fire, there wasn't much left of the portcullis or the heavy wooden doors. That had to be fixed right away. Fortunately, the royal carpenters were already at work.

On the other hand, the Head Gardener and a dozen under-gardeners in sturdy gray coveralls were moving rose bushes from one bed to another.

Someone had to tell them defenses took priority. As the only member of the family in Cochem, the princess made the attempt.

"Uh—"

"What are you standing around for?" The Head Gardener put down his bushel basket of flower bulbs and looked the princess up and down. "Pick up a shovel. Just look at this black ash everywhere—all those roses have to be moved before they die. The firefighters soaked the ground for us, people. Let's get these bulbs in."

Huh. The Head Gardener could have been more polite, but a castle fire was a stressful time, so the princess made allowances.

It was no time for a royal fuss.

"It's nice to save water, and those roses are beautiful, but . . ." She pointed up at the Tower. As soon as Queen Ash came back, they had to hold the castle against her and the Golden Parsnip. Those rose bushes would have to be bigger and nastier to slow her down at all.

A Sleeping Beauty hedge would be perfect. "Do you have some tall, thorny roses?"

"Tall, thorny roses?" The Head Gardener's lip curled. "*Bah!* These are the finest French roses, in honor of the christening of the youngest Cochem princess." His voice dropped to a tone of reverence. "They are called 'Le Bon Mot.' The name means 'the perfect word'."

This particular rose seemed a little silly since the princess never had the words she needed. For instance right now. But he'd gone to all this trouble.

The princess tried again. "A row of nice thorny, blackberry bushes in front . . . *uh*, here . . . would keep Queen Ash from . . . *um*, walking on—"

"Blackberries? This is a rose garden. Enough backtalk!" The Head Gardener shoved her towards a dozen under-gardeners.

"Aaaaah!" The princess lost her balance on the slippery ground and fell onto her hands. Her palms sank into the mud, and her face burned. No one had ever treated her like this before.

She went to wipe the mud off, remembered her brocade gown in the nick of time, and froze with her muddy hands in the air. Her gown was gone. She was wearing a gray coverall.

A shovel struck the ground next to her and bounced. Its handle smacked her in the head.

Ouch. She rubbed her head with the cleanest part of her arm. The mud might have been an accident, but the tool-throwing wasn't.

She wished her brothers and sisters were here. The Head Gardener needed a talking to. But he had already walked away.

Huh. As far as the princess knew, Cochem mud wasn't magical, so this must be *hiding in plain sight*. So far, her gift was convenient for wiping muddy hands, but likely to get you hit in the head. She wasn't impressed.

The under-gardener closest to the princess picked up her shovel and handed it to her. "You okay?"

Still recovering from the shock, the princess nodded and took the shovel. Nice to know under-gardeners took care of each other. Using one foot, she stepped her shovel into the ground and tossed a shovelful of dirt onto the pile.

Now that she thought about it, an extended moat wasn't the worst idea. Queen Ash wouldn't expect one over here.

One of the under-gardeners coughed, and the princess looked over.

Out of the Dishwater and Into the Storm

Crossing his arms on top of his shovel, the second under-gardener was inspecting her. "You know that bunch of evil blackberries? Down by the royal campgrounds?"

The princess nodded again. She'd helped Harold number three get his kite out of them once. But the Head Gardener didn't want blackberries.

"My wife makes jam every year," the first under-gardener called over. "I say we do it. The Head Gardener doesn't have to know everything."

The second under-gardener finished his section, but before he moved on to the next, he said, "We'll get'em when we're done. But I'm getting my heavy-duty gloves first."

These people understood things without too many words. She took a shuddery breath. They didn't know who she was, but they were helping her anyway. It made her proud of Cochem. They dug for a while in companionable silence.

From what the princess could see, the trench curved away from the castle. Taking her shovel, she followed the white line the under-gardeners were digging along as if she were looking for a new place to work. The line drew a perfect circle. She smacked her head with a muddy palm. Okay for a flowerbed, but useless as a moat.

Ever so casually, the princess picked up the lime bucket and brush and painted a straight line from the flowerbed to the existing moat. That should help.

The Head Gardener was laying out a complicated design in flower bulbs that seemed to be taking all his attention. The princess scraped out the old, curved line with her shovel and dug along her new line.

After a couple of hours, her palms burned and she had to

stop. The shovel certainly wasn't magical. It gave wicked blisters. And the flowerbed was still much too shallow for a moat.

With steady speed, the princess's old under-gardener friends caught up to her. She wondered how to get them to help her with this new problem.

The first under-gardener called across to the second under-gardener. "You always want blue and white gardens. What's wrong with a little color?"

The princess listened for an opening in the conversation.

"A little color, as an accent in a garden, yes. Planting rainbows of color in every bed isn't proper for a royal family." The second under-gardener punctuated his remark with a flying shovel of dirt.

"What kind of gardens do you like, then?" The first under-gardener asked the princess.

This was her chance. "*Uh.* Like . . . a moat?"

"A . . . what?" The second under-gardener laughed. "First blackberries and now a moat? You must have some friends you really don't want to see."

The princess choked out, "Queen Ash."

"Oh, ho! Blackfly repellent to the rescue." The first under-gardener chuckled. "A moat with lots of frogs."

Glomp! Glomp! Glomp! The second one opened and shut his mouth like a frog catching flies. "That'll manage the blackflies. I'm in."

"Me, too."

The princess wanted in too. She raised her hand. The under-gardeners gave her a high-five each and passed the word in both directions. The princess had to blink hard for a moment before she could dig again. She wasn't used to being seen. Catching sight of her gray coveralls, she reminded herself again that they didn't know who she was.

"Head Gardener wants a water garden." The first under-gardener passed the word as if it was a real command.

"Those water lilies want it DEEP. Dig, my hearties, dig!"

"A tall cold one afterwards at the Peppermint Tea House for all of you."

Groaning came from all sides, but the under-gardeners dug, and the shovels rang with the sound of dirt flying. Grateful for so much support, the princess dug until she couldn't lift another shovelful to save her life.

Saluting her colleagues in gray coveralls, she stepped out of the way of the professionals and went to find some firefighters. She needed water in the new moat right away. Not flowers. Queen Ash wasn't the kind to stop and smell the forget-me-nots.

In good weather, the Blackfly Kingdom was about a four-day journey from Cochem. Eight days wasn't a long time to put defenses into place. Walking up through the Tower's huge shadow, the princess worried they wouldn't finish in time. She'd already used up most of this day. Below the castle, the river valley lay half in shadow. The moat would need hours to fill. Fortunately, the princess knew where the off-duty Fire Chief spent his time. She turned the corner of the castle.

Armed with the fire hose, the Fire Chief was too busy waggling his eyebrows at Cook to pay attention to his work. Unfortunately, the water rushed right back out of the giant copper washtubs because no one had put the stoppers in. His large feet trampled the green parsnip tops into the mud.

The good news was she'd found the Fire Chief right where she thought he'd be. With Cook. That was also the bad news. How was the princess going to get him on the moat project instead?

Before the princess could open her mouth, Cook seized her. "There you are! Do you think christening dishes wash themselves?"

"The fire hose"–the princess was going to say, was needed to fill up the new moat, but Cook didn't wait.

"Isn't Chief lovely to help us when the kitchen is in such a state?" Cook simpered.

The Fire Chief bowed, overshooting the washtub and blasting the shaky tower of crockery with the water's force. He yanked the hose back, sideswiping the princess.

Splutter! She wiped the water from her face and arms. Oh well, it might help with the mud. When she looked down, the uniform she wore wasn't muddy at all. It was ... she wasn't sure what it was. She turned a smidgeon towards Cook, and it came into focus as a scullery maid uniform. The princess blinked. More magic.

"Get to work there." Cook pointed up at the tower of dishes.

First, the princess had to figure something out. She turned a fraction towards the Fire Chief and was instantly clad in a firefighter's waterproof coat with toggles.

Eyes fixed on the Fire Chief, Cook didn't seem to notice. Her arm still pointed uphill. "Dishes, I said."

Funny, the princess thought the toggles on her firefighter's coat were convincing. She'd have to test her gift the other way around. She turned to face the Fire Chief.

"Don't you have a pump to work, firefighter?" His stern

gaze swept over the princess, and he pointed towards the pump, downhill from the washtubs. "We need to get these washtubs filled."

The princess took a step closer to Cook, and the scullery maid uniform took over, complete with starched apron.

"Wait—where's my firefighter?" The Fire Chief narrowed his eyes. "A moment ago, she was standing right there."

He twirled around, spraying water 360 degrees. When the water hit Cook's ankles, she shrieked and jumped back, laughing.

The princess frowned and shook her head. What had her fairy godmother been thinking? How was a gift like this supposed to help govern a kingdom?

"What are you looking at?" Cook wasn't laughing now. She pointed the scullery maid princess towards the washtubs.

"It's the strain," Cook said to the Fire Chief. "Even a strong man needs care once in a while. Sit yourself down, and I'll get you something warm to drink."

The Fire Chief sat down while keeping the hose aimed at the washtubs.

Not bad.

"We know who's important around here." Cook snapped a playful dishcloth at him.

At this rate, the gardeners would have the moat full of flowers before the Fire Chief got back to work. Granted, he had worked all night to put the castle fire out.

The princess would have to fix things without words, the way she always did, *hiding in plain sight* or not. She hunted around in the grass for the stoppers and put them in the washtubs.

TROUBLE WITH PARSNIPS

After a few minutes, the washtubs filled.

Now for the moat. Counting on the Fire Chief only having eyes for Cook, the princess followed the hose back-a-ways, kinked it, and ran back up to the washtubs.

"Uh, no water, sir." The princess passed her hand back and forth in front of the nozzle.

As she'd hoped, he put the hose down to trace the problem but was held up by a few sweet nothings from Cook.

Staying well away from both, the princess swiveled the heavy pump on its stand, dragged it down the hill, and aimed the nozzle towards the new moat. Her long christening gown made it awkward. She braced herself for the water's rush and hoped no one noticed her gown.

"All clear!" the Fire Chief shouted, having apparently remembered his duty and checked the hose.

Now the hose was aimed in the right direction, but the princess couldn't stand here until the moat filled. She needed to get the Fire Chief to do it. Hopefully, the Fire Chief would feel like showing off his importance in front of Cook.

When he backed towards her, blowing farewell kisses at Cook, the princess dropped the hose and sprinted back up to him. Just as she'd hoped, her firefighter uniform came back.

Breathless, she saluted. "Sir—defenses, uh, are ... the moat needs more water." She pointed towards the muddy trench along the castle. Inspired by Cook, the princess burst out with, "They, uh, can't do it without you."

"This is where I leave you, ma'am." The Fire Chief twirled his mustaches at Cook and went back to working the fire hose, pulling the heavy pump behind him. As soon as he moved out of range, the princess's scullery maid outfit came back.

"Where have you been?" Cook gave the princess a stern look and marched back over to the outdoor bread oven.

Princesses were expected to help in any crisis, and the new moat was on track. The regular scullery maid, Bridget, wasn't around. She must be helping her father in the dungeon. Hungry firefighters and gardeners needed food and dishes to eat it from. A hungry castle was a vulnerable castle. The princess put on an apron and plowed into the suds.

A pity her fairy godmother hadn't picked a more practical gift, like magical feast-making or instant dishwashing. Or a magical way to make people understand what you needed them to know. This kind of work made her fingers prune-y and the blisters from the shovel burned in the soapy water. The princess washed three washtubs full of pots and climbed half inside the last huge stockpot to scrub the burned part at the bottom.

"Am I glad to see you!" It was a girl's voice, but not one of the Sibyls.

The princess hit her head on the pot getting out. And found herself eye-to-eye with the castle scullery maid who laughed and tossed the princess a clean dishtowel. "I'm Bridget, who are you?"

Uh. Since Bridget saw her constantly—on the way to and from the dungeon workshop—this was a strange question. At a moment like this, a name would come in handy. She could at least show her library card. "Uh. I'm the Fifteenth Child of Cochem."

TROUBLE WITH PARSNIPS

Bridget looked at her sideways. "Right, and I'm the Blackfly Queen. You don't look a thing like Fifteenth."

Fifteenth was what they called her because she didn't have a name. The princess ducked into the last pot to cover her confusion. This magical disguise hid her from people who talked to her every day? Did this mean her family wouldn't recognize her either?

Someone knocked on the side of the pot. "Helloooo?" Bridget called. "Why do you think we're washing all these pots? By now, the Fifteenth Child of Cochem has a name. And if you don't know what it is, you're not her."

Great logic. Too bad it wasn't true. The princess backed out of the pot and rinsed it with scalding water Cook had heated over the barbeque. Maybe Bridget would blame her red face on the heat.

Bridget took the pot, dumped the last water out and whipped it dry with her towel. "So, what do your friends call you?"

The princess pulled out the washtubs' plugs. Soapy water gurgled out onto the grass and flowed towards the vegetable garden. Fifteenth was the only "name" she'd ever had, and that wasn't going to work.

The princess shrugged and said nothing.

"Fine. I'll just call you Soapsuds until you tell me."

Dusk fell before the princess took off her soggy apron and followed Bridget over to a patch of drier grass. The light in the cloudy sky was going. Bridget opened her satchel and handed the princess a piece of cinnamon-dusted crumble cake.

Left over from the christening that hadn't happened.

Falling over on the grass, the princess ate her cake in

exhausted silence. Things looked bleak. Bridget fell asleep on the grass.

In front of them, the castle dripped from every parapet. The Tower's roof was gone. The stones under the castle windows were streaked with soot as if they'd been crying. Before they could defend the castle against Queen Ash, it had to be cleared for action.

Yawning, the princess forced her eyes to stay open. *Hiding in plain sight* was an exhausting way to look after the kingdom. She had to get help. If King Oliver and Queen Sibyl weren't well enough yet, she'd have to get whichever one of the Harolds or the Sibyls were. Even feverish, one of them could tell people what needed to be done.

In between wickets.

If they had a relapse, she could hand them a mallet. The princess told herself any one of them could take over from Queen Ash, as long as they didn't look Unfit.

They had to. It was too much for the princess.

She struggled to her hands and knees, but her eyes wouldn't stay open. She let her head rest on her hand for one moment.

CHAPTER FIVE
A Rocky Situation

The princess woke up, shivering, in the kitchen garden. The washtubs had been cleared away, and someone had thrown a tablecloth over her like a blanket. In the East, pink light battled with storm clouds.

Nooo! She'd slept the night away. Jumping up, she rubbed her arms with her hands and stamped her feet. She should be on her way to the Blackfly Kingdom to get whatever member of the Cochem royal family was healthiest. It didn't look like much of a plan, but it was what she had.

In the valley below, the Mosel River reflected the stormy sky. Its waters were a sulky gray.

Light in the castle kitchen window and clattering pans meant Cook was baking rolls for breakfast. The princess's stomach growled, but with her disguise, she couldn't risk the kitchen. She'd have to go without. She had to be back from the Blackfly Kingdom before Queen Ash, who already had a day's head start.

In real fairy tales, princesses got useful gifts, like Seven League Boots. Kizzy needed to do some remedial reading. The princess would just have to walk twice as fast.

A Rocky Situation

She crossed the garden and climbed the trail that led up through the vineyards. Black storm clouds built a fortress on top of the hills, and as she climbed up, she fought against the wind.

To her delight, her christening gown returned. It wasn't practical, but it was proof the party had happened, even if the christening hadn't. She'd never gotten so close to a name before. In spite of the wind, she walked along quite cheerfully for an hour, making good progress.

Suddenly, a brilliant flash lit the Cochem valley. Thunder boomed, rolling and rumbling until her whole body vibrated. *Uh oh!* She ran along the edge of the steep vineyard, looking for a storm shelter where she could wait it out.

The loose rocks on the path tripped her, and she caught her gown more than once on the stone terraces.

White rain sheeted down and blinded her. After a few ankle-deep puddles, her gown was muddy to the knee.

She splashed on for a while, getting soaked from every side. Then the trail doubled back on itself. She stopped. The shelter should have come before the switchback. She must have missed it. She backtracked, walking into the driving rain with her head down.

When she finally found it, the doorway was missing a few stones from its arch, but she ducked inside anyway, sopping wet and breathing hard.

Rain beat against the ground as if it would never stop. At first, it was a relief. There were worse places to wait out a storm.

Trickles of water grew into rivulets. A waterfall filled the doorway, and the constant sound made it hard to tell how long she'd been there.

She shivered in the cold, wished for Númi's horse blanket, and hoped her family had reached shelter. Croquet in this weather could be hazardous to your health. Also, the Blackfly Kingdom wasn't known for dry tents.

It must have been hours later when she went to the doorway to see if the storm was slacking off. Lightning flashed nearby, and the accompanying thunder made her wait a little longer. The rain lashed down as if someone had turned a valve all the way open.

Trying to fix the stonework of the shelter, she pushed a stone in, and two stones came loose.

Clunk, clunk!

Ohhhh. She grabbed her foot and held it against the pain. More stones fell from the arch above, pelting her head. She had to get out of here.

The rest of the doorway fell in with a crash.

"Ow!" She fell back and found herself in the pitch dark.

It couldn't be. She must have her eyes closed. She blinked. No difference. Reaching forward in the dark, she ran her hands over the stones until she found one that wiggled. She yanked with all her strength. Dirt and rocks rolled down from the inside walls of the shelter. More rocks bounced on her foot.

"Ouch, ouch, ouch." She touched the hurt place, and her hand came away sticky. *Ick.* She was bleeding and trapped.

No one knew she was here. Her whole family was in the Blackfly Kingdom and hadn't missed her. Her eyes smarted. She'd just run off into the dark as if any of her fourteen siblings were only a shout away. What had she been thinking?

A Rocky Situation

Stop. She was a Cochem princess. It was her duty to go for help. This was a busy vineyard path. When the vintners came to prune the vines, they would walk right by. No, they wouldn't–the spring pruning was done. The vintners had groomed all the vineyards early, in honor of her christening.

She breathed in.

She breathed out.

Hugh didn't approve of panic attacks. He said, "You must think things through."

She blinked the water out of her eyes. A blueprint. As soon as she had a plan, she would know what to do.

Queen Ash had inspired the Cloud of Defense. She could inspire a few more inventions. The princess closed her eyes because that made it easier to pretend she was taking stock in her dungeon workshop.

Okay, she wasn't on her way to the Blackfly Kingdom, so the Cochem-family-replacement-for-the-Regent project was . . . stalled.

Outside, lightning flashed even through the tiny chinks, and an immediate, tremendous boom followed.

Too close.

After the lightning, it looked even darker in the shelter. She moved quickly on to the next problem: castle defenses. How were they doing so far?

Wait–the storm was filling up the new moat. Ridiculously cheered, she started a "progress" list in her head:

One A: Moat. Check.

French roses with fancy names might not like lots of rain, but the under-gardeners had promised to plant some wild blackberries. In weather like this, wild blackberries would grow thorns three inches long. Queen Ash's long black gown would catch on every branch. That should slow her down.

One B: Sleeping beauty hedges. Check.

The defense project was in good shape.

Two A: Shelter from the storm. Check. Her breath got quivery, so she made a giant check in the air with her whole arm. Check.

Two B: Getting-to-the-Blackfly-Kingdom. No check. Keeping up morale was more important than solutions. Until the storm stopped, she was NOT going to think about being trapped in here.

That left the name problem. After ten years of trying, it seemed harder, not easier. If King Oliver and Queen Sibyl were home and healthy on the 15th, the Speech Tournament would pull them away from the princess's problem.

Some people would say the Tournament was the perfect chance to get a name. All Seven Kingdoms would already be there, trying to win the Velvet Purse. A big prize like that was worth traveling for. Once the Bishop had an invitation, the princess would be set, right?

Hugh Ancry would say, "Right." Once they got over their croquet fever, all her brothers and sisters would too.

But the princess knew better. She could raise and train twice as many goldfish. Her parents wouldn't gaze in the moat, notice a banner flying from the Tower, or stroll by a series of limericks posted in the gardens.

Queen Ash had the Golden Parsnip, but she wouldn't use it for the Tournament. At the last-minute, King Oliver and Queen Sibyl would have to make the beds, order the food, pay the bills, and build the speaking platform.

If the princess got out of here—

A Rocky Situation

Stop!

Deep breath.

WHEN she got out of here, she could make beds, after she'd solved the defense problem and brought at least one healthy member of her family back to Cochem.

But guests from the Seven Kingdoms had all kinds of emergencies. Who knew how many of her brothers and sisters would be "on deck" to help? The sick ones couldn't.

The healthy ones would practice their speeches, adjust their outfits all over the castle, and leave trails of colorful index cards all over the place.

No—during the Tournament—the only way to get anyone's attention was to give an absolutely spell-binding, emotional, roller-coaster of a speech. Prince Nero gave one every year.

But the princess wasn't a speaker like her brothers and sisters. A speech asking her parents to give her a name?

Ha!

Once she stood up in front of people, she forgot she didn't have one.

Opening her eyes, she stared into the dark. She had to face facts. The name problem had no solution. She couldn't give a moving speech.

A sharp pinch in her stomach reminded her she hadn't eaten since the night before. Facing facts was bad for morale.

Quick—she needed something cheerful to think about. Dessert sluices. No, not food. Cable ferries?

Yes, ferries—those were cheerful. A little boat that ran from one side of the river to the other would be the perfect way to get to the Blackfly Kingdom in a hurry. If a steel cable connected one side of the Mosel River to the other, you could somehow hook a ferry onto that cable. The cable wouldn't let the ferry go downstream, so the current's strength pushed the ferry sideways. She took another deep breath, and it wasn't quite as shuddery as before. Ferries helped.

In January, she'd built a tiny ferry for the moat. But before King Oliver could look at it, Harold number three fell into the moat, accidentally-on-purpose, to get out of a math test. The ferry hadn't survived, and Harold number three's cold had traveled through the entire family all winter. Queen Sibyl had been anti-ferry ever since.

Not that it mattered, since the princess might be here for the rest of her life.

Stop.

The bitter taste in her mouth was only the dust. Dust meant the shelter was keeping out the rain. What else?

At least Kizzy's gift couldn't make this worse. The princess wasn't in anyone's plain sight. She couldn't be any less visible than she already was. Her fingers itched to pull the rocks out and make the wall stable, but it was too risky, dust or no dust.

In the morning, someone had to come by, and she'd make them hear, even if it took an avalanche to get their attention.

*****

Much later, a rook's cry startled the princess awake. Her mouth tasted like the bottom of the moat but the rain must have stopped. The rock pile between her and the outside world glowed pink with the morning light.

Then she heard voices and laughter taking turns. People

A Rocky Situation

walking together talked like that, and they were getting louder.

The princess cleared her dusty throat, and her body, misunderstanding, stabbed her with an urgent demand for food.

Ow! Doubling over, she grabbed her stomach, but the voices sounded so near. It was now or never. She called out, "The wall fell in, and I'm traaaapped in this shelter. Help me!"

Something was wrong with her voice.

"Did you hear that?" A man's voice.

He'd heard. The princess's heart beat faster. She was saved, and as soon as they got her out, she could have a drink of water. A convenient bush wouldn't be bad either.

"Did I hear that?" A woman laughed. "You did that yourself. 'Help me, I'm traaaapped!' is the oldest ventriloquist's trick in the book."

The princess's voice might sound a little odd, but that was just the stone all around her. She called out again. "Help!"

The man said, "Admit it, Hildy, it was you."

Huh. The princess hopped from one foot to the other. She shouted, "I'm not aaaaa ventriloquist, I'm the Fifteenth Child of Cochem."

Did *hiding in plain sight* mess with her voice when no one could see her? Kizzy deserved to lose her fairy godmother license.

She shrieked, "I'd reaaaaally appreciate it if you'd help me out. I need to go rescue my faaamily from the Blaaaackfly Kingdom."

The crunching stopped. "Oh, that's nicely done, I'll admit

it," the man said. "The littlest princess is aaa nice touch. Everyone knows what aaa prankster she is. I knew you were good, but I never knew how good until now."

"Don't you dare pretend that wasn't your voice, Darnell Brummer! Your long A's are a dead giveaway," Hildy said. "No royal princess speaks like a vintner, even if she is a prankster. They can't do it. That was you, I know it."

The princess stamped a foot in frustration. These ventriloquists were so busy impressing each other with their talking that they weren't listening at all.

The vintners started off again, their feet scuffing the trail.

"Waaaaait! Please waaaaait! I aaam aaaaa Cochem princess, and I've got to get out of here." She sounded like a vintner. Her brothers and sisters were right. Fairy godmothers were nothing but trouble.

"Okay, you've got to tell me how you're doing that," Darnell said.

Hildy's laughter faded into the distance. The princess sat down on her rocks and crossed her legs.

If she ever got out of here, she was paying a visit to the Vintner's Ventriloquism League with the entire royal family. And the royal archers. For emphasis.

For a long time afterwards, birdsong was the only sound. No one was on their way to work. A little more light filtered through the chinks. At this time, there should be much more foot traffic.

Farmers should be driving wagons into the valley to spread manure. Seed merchants should be carrying rucksacks full of parsnip, carrot, pea, bean, and cucumber seeds to sell in the valley. If King Oliver ever offered her a kingdom-wide holiday in her honor again, she would turn it

A Rocky Situation

down.

Desperate now, she pried a rock free, only to have more rocks shower down between her and the outside world. Coughing and choking, she wiped her eyes on her sleeve.

She'd always known she would grow up, and someday her fourteen siblings wouldn't be around to ask for help, but she'd never thought that time would come so soon. Croquet fever had taken her whole family away at once.

The princess crossed her legs the other way around and rocked miserably back and forth. She had to get out of here so she could see them all again.

CHAPTER SIX
A Princely Rescue

OUTSIDE, SOMEONE WAS whistling the tune to "*How can I keep from singing?*"

The princess stopped rocking. "Hello?"

The whistling stopped.

The princess called out again. "Can you hear me?" Without those extra long A's, her voice sounded more like herself. Was it one of her siblings after all?

The gravel crunched louder and faster.

"Who's there? In the name of Nero, Prince of the Blackfly Kingdom—"

Uh oh. The Blackflys were the wrong rescuers. The princess couldn't believe it. How could Queen Ash be back already? She'd barely been gone two days.

"—I charge you to tell me your name!"

Explaining why the princess didn't have one would take much too long. "Can that wait? I've been here all night." She yanked a rock out of the pile and then another and another, imagining the damage Queen Ash could do in the eight days the princess needed to get her family home. For the umpteenth time, she wondered why Kizzy couldn't have given her a useful gift.

A shower of rocks sent her back from the entrance, coughing and wiping her eyes. When the dust cleared, Nero's head was visible. Not bad. A cloud of blackflies flew into the shelter, confirming his identity beyond a doubt.

Nero peered in at her. "You sound so familiar."

She wished he'd focus on the rocks. "We've met." She pulled at another rock and made a new dirt waterfall. Even with both arms over her face, grit showered into her eyes.

From the sound of it, Nero had gotten back to moving rocks. After a few minutes, his hand came through the opening. "That should do it. Need a hand?"

"*Uh*, no, thanks." The princess hoisted herself over the rock pile into the blinding daylight. She squinted and blinked, trying to make her eyes work. Nero wore black boots, black pants, and a black traveling cloak. Two others were dressed to match. Was King Schwartz here too? Queen Ash in trousers seemed impossible.

Bobbing a curtsy, the princess noticed her gown had turned black. *Right*. Her magical disguise took its job much too seriously.

She shaded her eyes with both hands. Nero and two Blackfly archers. She spun around to make sure. "*Uh*– where's Queen Ash?"

"On her way to the Blackfly Kingdom, the last time I looked." Nero's smile wasn't quite a smirk.

Hopping from one foot to the other, the princess gestured towards the nearest thicket. "If you don't mind– *uh*, could we chat some other time?"

"Oh." He turned abruptly. "I'll be over there. Archers!" He pointed towards the stone wall that kept the next vineyard from sliding down into the valley. He and his archers marched off together.

The princess went behind the bushes and came out a few minutes later, much relieved. Now she was only hungry, thirsty, and in need of information. She headed down to Nero.

"You don't look so good." He rummaged in his black backpack, pulled out a flask, and gave it to her. "Drink this. Don't worry—I didn't drink out of it."

Her mouth was too dry to speak. After a drink, the information gathering was going to be much less painful. She put it to her mouth, tipped her head back, and the clean, cool, peppermint tea poured into her mouth. She swallowed a quarter of it before she could make herself stop, gasping for air. She held it out to him. "Thank you."

"Keep it." He rummaged again and handed her a hunk of brown bread. "Here."

Not bread, rock-hard gingerbread. While she gnawed on it, she walked, trying to make up for lost time. Actually, this stuff wasn't bad. King Oliver should require every shelter to have emergency gingerbread.

"What are you doing in the Cochem Kingdom all by yourself?" Nero asked.

A dumb question for a boy whose mother set Cochem Castle on fire. "Croquet fever?"

"So you thought you'd put yourself in quarantine?" Nero pointed back at the shelter.

Having seven brothers gave a girl skills. She withered him with a look.

"Sorry, sorry." Nero threw his hands in the air. "But seriously, Blackfly princesses don't visit the Seven

Kingdoms every day. Oh." His face cleared. "You were here for the christening?"

A magical disguise made it complicated to talk to people. You had to keep thinking about who they thought you were. The princess nodded.

"That's no way to treat a guest," Nero said. "It's a huge family. Nobody remembered you while waiting their turn? Unbelievable. What if I hadn't gotten lost on my way back? You'd still be trapped."

The princess's smile evaporated. Nero was right. Even after the 500 synchronized-spelling goldfish, her family had forgotten her. She needed something bigger. The dessert fountain was bigger, but not something her family saw every day, so they forgot her in between. She blinked hard a few times.

"Did you get dirt in your eyes?" Nero offered her a handkerchief.

A pristine, black, neatly pressed handkerchief. The princess sputtered, but even that helped her hold herself together. A very effective handkerchief, in its own way. "Uh, no, thanks."

"Next time, come straight to the Blackfly Kingdom. We take much better care of our guests."

The princess choked. Weren't the only "guests" in the Blackfly Kingdom the ones who hadn't paid their tolls? Or had croquet fever?

Nero pounded her on the back, and she held up her hand for him to stop. She still needed a sibling for back-up, and she needed to know what Queen Ash was up to. Nothing had changed.

"I've got it—Melanie!" Nero said.

Neither of the Blackfly archers looked up, and they were the only other people on the trail.

"What?" the princess asked.

"Took me a while." Nero smiled at her. "I knew you were my cousin from Minnesota, but I couldn't remember your name before. Melanie is right, isn't it?" He looked a little worried.

"*Uh, no.*" *Melanie?* The princess blinked. That was a new one.

"So if your name isn't Melanie, what is it?" A challenge, not a question.

"Uh, the castle burned down before we got to the . . . name part."

"Mmmm. Sorry to hear that." He held up an index finger. "Look at my finger—I want to see if your pupils are the same size." He moved his finger slowly from left to right.

Hello? The princess glared at him. She was getting tired of not being heard. Christenings with castle fires weren't a regular thing in the Seven Kingdoms. Neither were ten-year-old nameless princesses. Her magical disguise trumped all of those "little" details, but she didn't want it to win. "Some people call me, *uh*, . . . Fifteenth."

"Pleased to meet you, Fifteenth." He hadn't missed a beat, and his eyes were distant. Almost automatic. Had he even heard her?

His gaze shifted to the top of her head. After dirt showering down all night, she didn't want to know what was in her hair. She was on a strategic strike mission to bring back a sibling. Enough. She turned her back on him and headed down the path.

A moment later, he poked the back of her head.

A Princely Rescue

"Hey!" She whirled around, but kept walking.

"Sorry." He kept pace.

He was still looking at her like a problem to solve, so maybe her disguise wasn't actually good enough to fool people who were paying attention. That would be okay with her.

Something bit her in the neck. "*Ow!*"

Darn that Kizzy!

Nero swatted and missed. "You even have your own blackflies. But they don't usually bite us." Frowning, he inspected her neck. "I know. You were on your way to visit us when you got hit in the head and forgot who you were."

Uh, no. She knew exactly who she was. Without a name though, you had to tell people your life's story. Introducing yourself got tiring. "I've lived here since I was born. I'm ten. I'm a Cochem princess—"

"Look at you—you could be my twin sister. And even if you looked like a Cochem princess, you couldn't be one." Nero made a sweeping gesture from her black princess pointy cone hat to her black princess shoes. "They're all in the Blackfly Kingdom, playing croquet."

"Wait, Queen Ash was playing too?" The princess stopped dead. Queen Ash with croquet fever would solve everything.

"*Nah.*" Nero wrinkled his nose. "She was putting a listing on AirCastle."

AirCastle—whatever that was—didn't sound weighty enough to keep Queen Ash at home. A pity she hadn't caught croquet fever.

Nero was still raving about the Blackfly Kingdom. "You'll love our castle. The galleries go all the way around the inner courtyard on every floor." He sketched them in the air with his hands. "If you set up the hoops just right, a whole course fits perfectly. We have the hoops with the wooden feet that work on stone floors. They are probably playing all three levels now. When you get to the bottom, you start over at the top."

Ouch. Her family and three levels of never ending croquet. The princess groaned. But wait—Nero had walked away from the game. "How did you, *uh*, get over it so fast?"

"Oh, I never got it. Don't worry, they'll still be playing when you get there," Nero said. "On the way there, they weren't even slowing down."

The rock settled back in the princess's stomach. No one in her family was going to be able to help her. She was going to have to defend Cochem Castle all by herself.

"That's why Queen Ash sent me back to Cochem."

"Sent you back?" The princess hoped that meant Queen Ash would take her time. As an invader, Nero seemed less intimidating.

"The Queen commands, the Prince is her foot soldier." He shuffled a step sideways and back, the way Harold number one did when he was trying not to show off. "Crown Prince assignment. Reporting for duty in the Cochem Kingdom." He saluted.

"You mean she gave you the Golden Parsnip?" The princess's hands flew to her hips.

"Hey—of course not." Nero took a step back. "Handoffs are against the law."

"Oh. Sorry." The princess hadn't known the law mattered to anyone in the Blackfly Kingdom.

The moment passed and Nero shrugged. "How could you

know? You're not from here. And your last hosts didn't take very good care of you."

Fine. Let him think she was some Blackfly princess. He had evidently decided to walk her back to the border. Misplaced chivalry was okay with her. The longer he spent walking away from the Cochem Kingdom, the longer the blackberry brambles could grow.

The Blackfly archers trailed behind. Without Queen Ash around, they seemed a lot more relaxed. One had tied a black handkerchief to the end of his bow and was catching butterflies as they went along.

They walked the whole afternoon in the sun, with a breeze blowing the grassy meadow around them, as if the storm and the castle fire had never been.

The princess mentioned hot air balloons, and Nero asked a million questions. As if she were a regular person with a name. It would have been one of the nicest afternoons in her life if she hadn't had to spend every moment figuring out how to defend her family's home until they got back.

At its highest point above the Mosel River, the trail broadened out into a road on a wide, level plain. They walked along, side-by-side, and the princess wondered if a castle swap could break up the croquet game. If paying guests came, Queen Ash might send the Cochem family home. "What's *uh*, a castle swap?"

"Castle swap? You put up a listing." Nero glanced over at her. "You know, 'Get *away from it all in our family castle on the water, good hearth, minimal toll-collecting duties, on-site bakery, water dungeon, rugged landscape with showy purple thistles.*' That sort of thing."

"Showy. Purple. Thistles." The princess choked, again.

TROUBLE WITH PARSNIPS

"Rugged. Landscape." Blackfly Castle was a boat-shaped fortress on a pile of rocks in the middle of the river.

Nero folded his arms and looked down at her sideways. "I thought it was pretty good."

The princess wished she had the right words, but showy thistles were a challenging topic. "Won't it be hard to find people who want to take over your toll-collecting?"

"Nah, it makes their vacation that much cheaper."

She couldn't imagine it, but the Seven Kingdoms had all kinds of people. "So where are you going to live while the Blackfly Castle's rented out?"

"Oh, that's my assignment in Cochem," Nero said, offhandedly. "To get it ready for the family."

The princess couldn't have heard him right. "The Blackfly family?"

"Of course. Queen Ash promised to look after Cochem Kingdom. That's why she has the Golden Parsnip. Did you miss that part?" Nero sounded altogether too patient.

No, the princess hadn't missed that part. She'd been a bit busy. The Golden Parsnip was for planning a Tournament—not a TakeOver—but then Queen Ash had crossed her fingers behind her back.

Blackberry brambles weren't going to be enough.

So far Kizzy's gift had only caused trouble, but it was supposed to help the princess govern the kingdom. If Nero was taking over the castle, it was time to test it out. The princess took a deep breath and tried to sound unconcerned as if she really were some Melanie person from Minnesota. "Uh, so how long is a castle swap?"

"Well, once it's comfortable, we can stay as long as we like." Nero smiled. "You're invited too."

An invitation to stay in her own castle as a Blackfly. She'd be sleeping in her own dungeon next.

"That's funny," Nero pointed to a trail sign marking the border of the Cochem Kingdom. "Somebody turned the sign around."

Thank you for visiting Cochem Kingdom! Come again soon! Other than being a little too welcoming to Blackfly invaders, the sign was fine. The princess didn't get it.

One Blackfly archer snorted, and the other one coughed. The princess frowned at them for laughing at Nero's mistake.

"What?" Nero said, turning on his archers. "Okay, so which way is the Cochem Kingdom then?"

With blank faces, the Blackfly archers pointed towards Cochem, back in the direction they'd just come. The princess would have gladly pointed the other way, but Nero arriving back in the Blackfly Kingdom would mean Queen Ash in Cochem even sooner.

There was only one thing to do. The princess had to take Nero back to Cochem and get in his way as much as she could as a fake Blackfly, chatting as much as possible. A terrible plan.

Nero walked all the way around the sign. "I don't get why this happens to me."

His forehead wrinkled, and the princess suddenly understood. She felt exactly the same way about podiums at the Speech Tournament. "You probably got turned around when you helped me out of the shelter."

His face cleared. "Right, that must have been it."

"I think you can send them home now." She looked at the archers. "It's safe in Cochem." As long as Queen Ash wasn't visiting.

"They help me out when I get lost."

The princess wasn't convinced. "We won't get lost."

"If you say so." Nero dismissed them.

Two fewer Blackfly subjects to worry about.

A few hours later, Cochem Castle was finally in sight. Cochem urgently needed a drier, easier way to get to and from the Blackfly Kingdom.

"Wouldn't the Tower would be perfect for a hot-air balloon launch?" she asked Nero, trudging along beside her.

He hadn't said much for the last hour, and now he only glanced in the direction she was pointing. "Might be easier if it had a roof."

Well, whose fault was that?

The Tower would still have a roof if she hadn't passed herself off as a Blackfly prince. Was passing herself off as a Blackfly princess really the wisest thing? Who knew what might happen?

CHAPTER SEVEN

Charming Complications

THE PRINCESS TOOK Nero the shortest way down to the castle since she wanted to get to work on the castle defenses right after they got something to eat. The first rule of surviving any siege was "Don't Starve." They'd wasted the whole day walking back and forth, and it was suppertime. Rock hard gingerbread didn't have much staying power.

The second rule was "Don't Let Your Enemy Know Your Secret Weak Points." Making conversation was hard enough with a disguise. So far, he hadn't seen through it. Once he did, working on defenses while pretending to "help" him with renovations was going to be a lot harder. Nero could fix up the castle—it would keep him out of her way—but Queen Ash wasn't taking it over.

Assuming the moat and the blackberry bushes were ready-to-go, the princess could move on to the next layer of defense. She decided to lock up everything lockable, starting with the Palace Agricultural Library.

With the Golden Parsnip, Queen Ash could demand the keys, but she couldn't have them if no one knew where they were. After today, the keys would be in the princess's pocket, not hanging on a hook in the hall. She might as well make use of her forgetability.

To the princess's great pleasure, her clothes stayed black even when they entered Cook's domain. No danger of dishwashing. There was a momentary flicker, a ghost of a scullery maid's apron, and then Nero caught up to her, and she looked like a Blackfly princess. She congratulated herself. Nero as a smokescreen would make things much easier.

The comforting scent of thyme drove out every other thought. Cook was supervising a huge cauldron of French lentil soup with potatoes and carrots. The princess's stomach clenched. She opened her mouth to ask for soup but Cook picked up the poker and brandished it in a way that would have impressed all seven Cochem princes.

"Uh . . ." The princess's words died. This was the flip side of her disguise.

Nero stepped in front of her and introduced himself with a formal bow. "Sorry to burst in on you, ma'am. I was just coming to see what could be done about the terrible castle fire. King Schwartz sent me to see if I can help. Hope you don't mind if I say that soup smells absolutely marvelous."

To the princess's amazement, Cook put her poker away, saying, "Well, a prince can't help where he's born, can he?" She bustled around and gave him—but not the princess—a spoon and a bowl of soup.

Nero took the soup and inclined his head in a mini-bow of thanks. Cook blushed and gave him a piece of bread to go with it. The princess was fascinated and a little disturbed.

"You won't want to eat in the hall," Cook held her nose and shook her head.

Charming Complications

Nero passed the bowl of soup to the princess. "After we eat, we'll go see what needs doing."

Cook frowned, but made him another bowl.

The princess breathed in the thyme-scented steam rising from her bowl. The first moment or two had been rocky, but Nero was helping things along. Checking out the hall fit perfectly into the princess's retrieve-the-keys plan. With a Blackfly prince, her disguise got her soup. Without one, it got her sinks full of pots and pans.

She also needed to check on the castle's best fire protection, the dessert sluice. Lost in her plans, she spooned soup absently into her mouth.

"*Ow, ummmm, ah!*" Her eyes watered. The soup was boiling.

"And who are you?" Cook reached for the poker again, apparently taking the princess's reaction as an insult.

The princess waved her arms apologetically and hopped around trying to cool the soup in her mouth so she could swallow. Being overlooked was more comfortable.

Nero's eyebrows came together, and his elbows stuck out like a bristling porcupine. "How is it, ma'am, that you don't recognize my cousin?"

Here it came. The princess swallowed and took another spoonful of soup, blowing on it first. If she had to be unmasked, she'd rather have a full stomach.

"She's been here as a guest for ten years." He sounded like he took it personally.

Huh. Now he thought she'd been here as a Blackfly from Minnesota for ten years? Where was he getting this stuff?

Cook's manner stiffened. "No disrespect, sir, but no Blackfly princesses live here."

The princess was sure Nero would catch on, but he gave her a half-smile that vanished when he turned towards Cook. "Let me be the first to introduce your guest."

Nero was a polite prince but a few parsnips short of a bushel.

Handing the princess forward, Nero introduced her with a voice like iced knives. "This. Is. My. Cousin. Princess Fifteenth."

The princess choked. There were only seven Cochem princesses. She wasn't going to explain that she was the Fifteenth Child of Cochem but only the eighth princess. He would only call her Princess Eighth or something even more ridiculous.

"You Blackfly Royals think you're so clever." Cook's eyes narrowed. "Taking names that belong to other people is impertinent. That's what it is. Especially if you get them wrong. Of course, now that the christening's over, she has a new one. Not that I've heard what it is yet."

Cook had just stood up for Fifteenth . . . against a "Blackfly princess." *Unbelievable.* And heartwarming.

Cook put the lid on the soup pot and reached for the princess's bowl. "I should take that back from you."

Jumping back, the princess shoveled in carrots and potatoes and lentils at top speed.

On the other hand, if everyone came after the princess with pokers, life in the castle was going to be much harder. She chased the last escape-ist carrot until she got it on her spoon and then Cook's lovely soup was gone. "Thank you," she said, but Cook didn't hear. Reluctantly, the princess set her spoon and bowl on the drainboard. She would have washed it herself, but staying near the dishes felt too risky.

Charming Complications

Nero cleared his throat and offered his empty soup bowl to Cook. "This is the best soup I've ever tasted." He must have decided Cook had been punished enough.

Cook stopped staring at the princess and bustled about for an even bigger bowl of soup. Hand on his chin, Nero looked over at the princess. "I wonder how I got the name wrong."

Huh. He'd introduced her that way on purpose, pounding her on the back almost before she had choked. He might have noticed something. Or *hiding in plain sight* made him mush all the "facts" together.

She'd have to be careful. She needed her magical disguise to get the defenses in place.

Cook chose that moment to give Nero his seconds. He made her a graceful bow, waving his spoon in the air like a virtuoso. "The most excellent soup in the Seven Kingdoms."

Cook beamed and offered him another ladleful. She ignored the princess.

The princess could deal. She was counting on Queen Ash ignoring her too. While Cook and Nero were occupied, the princess put the poker on the far side of the hearth, to prevent further misunderstandings. When Nero had finished his compliments, they went out to the hall.

Wet ashes, mildew, and burnt wood made the princess gag. Rushes squelched under their feet. The damage was even worse than she'd thought.

Nero went straight to the walls, tapping the stones, and wiggling the banner holders.

Fire safety was crucial and, for the princess, that meant the dessert sluice. She crawled underneath a sluiceway to check the mechanism, following its path around the hall. It needed cleaning, oil, and new pieces welded on, where the heat had warped its shape. She frowned, wondering how she was going to get it fixed before Queen Ash showed up.

She opened the cupboard with the dessert sluice controls. Her keys hung on the hook, but the wooden levers, swollen with water, were jammed.

On the other end of the hall, Nero tugged at a charred banner, and it crumbled under his fingers.

"We have to replace the banners, anyway."

The princess looked from Nero to the burnt banners and back. "Anyway?"

He shrugged. "They're the wrong color."

"Ahhh." She bit her lip. For a moment, she'd forgotten they weren't on the same side.

"Does this kind of thing happen a lot?"

The princess gritted her teeth. "Only when the Blackfly family shows up."

"Because people from Minnesota like to set fires?" Nero nudged the hearth ashes with his foot. "I heard it's cold there."

"Not me." This was her chance to get the Blackflies to stop picking fights with some cousinly advice. "You know, if the Blackflys, I mean, if your part of our Blackfly family didn't come late all the time, they wouldn't miss the food."

Nero cleared his throat. "A host waits until the guests arrive."

"The host waited. And so did all the other guests. For hours. The parsnip fries were getting soggy." The princess waited for Nero's reaction. A person's views on parsnip fries could tell you a lot about them.

"Okay, but the Blackfly Kingdom has the farthest to go to

Charming Complications

get here. How punctual do they want us to be? I mean, did King Oliver look at his watch and say, "That's it, it's one minute after, we're starting now?" A thoughtful look came over Nero's face. "That's another thing. Why did King Oliver say I'd arrived at the feast hours before?"

This was getting awkward, but she wanted to know how strong this magic was. For when Queen Ash showed up. How close could the princess get to the truth before Nero figured it out?

"Oh, *uh*, that part." The princess put herself in the place of an imaginary Blackfly princess at a Cochem princess's christening feast. "The Cochem family has lots of royal children."

"Yep." Nero nodded.

"And the youngest one didn't get christened for ten years." Somehow she had to change the topic.

Nero nodded again. He knew that too.

"So I didn't think, *uh* . . . she should wait longer."

Nero's nod was slower this time, and his eyes held a question.

Then it came to her. His Minnesota cousin could rescue the youngest princess of Cochem. Why not? It was the simplest story to keep track of because it was almost the truth. "So I dressed up like you and rode into the hall."

Grinding the rushes with the heel of his shoe, Nero frowned.

He'd figured it out. The princess braced herself.

When he looked up, there was a dangerous look in his eyes. "They didn't recognize you."

Okay, he hadn't. The princess pursed her lips. No reason to get her feelings hurt just because he was looking right at her. She didn't want him to recognize her. She forced a smile. "Well, even you said I looked just like you. I was hungry."

"Hungry?" He reached down, ripped some burnt and soggy rushes loose, and whipped them into the corner. "That's why Cook didn't recognize you. They starved you."

She wondered what it felt like if someone defended you when they knew who you were. "Don't be ridiculous. They never starved me. I didn't want the other kingdoms to be angry at the Blackfly Kingdom."

Rubbing his hands clean, Nero looked up at her with respect. "You know that's diplomatic thinking. We're a great team."

The princess swallowed. Until he figured out she was a fake.

"Hey, what's going on in there?" boomed a voice from the kitchen. The massive Fire Chief strode into the hall, and his big boots clomped on the dais. "I don't know what you Blackfly people think you're doing here. You've already caused enough trouble."

Uh, oh. Cook had evidently sent for help.

Glowering at Nero, the Fire Chief put his hands on his hips. "I must ask you to leave."

Counting on Nero to run interference, the princess slipped over to the cupboard and quietly took down her keys. She shut the cupboard door, but the motion must have caught the Fire Chief's attention. He strode over to her. "What do you think you're doing, little lady? Hand over those keys. They don't belong to you."

He grabbed them right out of her hand.

To secure the castle, she had to have those. She jumped

towards him, reaching for the keys, but missed.

Nero leapt over the smoldering hearth fire and ran across to help, but he was too late.

The Fire Chief had already fastened the princess's keys on his huge key ring and tucked it away inside his uniform." Grabbing the princess by the arms, he tossed her out through the open door.

Flying through the air, she passed through the doorway and landed on hands and knees in wet, squishy stuff. *Ick.* She decided it was rain-blasted peony petals, whether it was or not.

Nero must have gotten the same treatment, but didn't fly as far. Right in front of the castle entrance, he hit the gravel with a gritty crunch.

Judging from the sound, it must have hurt, but he didn't cry out. After a moment, he said, "That didn't go so well."

The Fire Chief shouted up to the gatekeeper, and the portcullis came down, creaking and squeaking, before either Nero or the princess could slip back inside. Normally, Cochem wasn't a close-the-portcullis-at-dusk kind of kingdom.

If Kizzy had been anywhere near the peonies, the princess would have had some strong words about magical christening gifts. But there was no sign of her. The princess shoved the portcullis with her hands, but it didn't budge. The rough repair with old boards was too strong.

Picking gravel out of his palm, Nero came over to help. The good news: the portcullis was solid enough to slow Queen Ash down a little. The bad news: the princess needed to be on the other side.

"Too bad he took the keys," Nero said. "Any secret

passages in Cochem?"

"Nope." They'd never needed one before. The blueprint collection in the Palace Agricultural Library might be worth checking. Not that she'd tell a Blackfly if she found anything.

The closest she'd ever come to a secret passage was a fake wall she'd sketched to protect her tools from her brothers. She'd never built it. "We'll have to sleep in the dungeon."

But when they went around the castle, the dungeon access was locked too. On the grounds that the portcullis might open at daybreak, they camped in front of it.

"The grass is wet." While the princess was glad someone was paying attention to security, she'd been looking forward to her cushy silver sleeping bag. First thing tomorrow, she had to get her keys.

"That's okay." Nero settled himself on the gravel with a sigh of contentment. In the Blackfly Kingdom, a gravel bed was probably a spa treatment.

"Hmmm." The princess shifted her head back and forth, trying to find a spot that didn't dig into her scalp. Was her family comfortable in the Blackfly Kingdom? Were they getting healthier?

CHAPTER EIGHT
Speaking Clearly with Tact Is an Art

AT FIRST LIGHT, the princess struggled to her feet. Her body felt like armor hammered with a million tiny dents. Her next night's sleep was going to be rock free.

The castle's main Tower had gaping holes in its roof, but it would take more than that to keep Hugh Ancry out of the Palace Agricultural Library. If she could get a message to him, he would let her back into the castle.

Or would he? No one had seen through her disguise so far. Even though Hugh always had time for her, he wouldn't be different. He was a librarian, not a magician.

Nero lay on the gravel, smiling in his sleep, probably dreaming of kingdom takeovers. The princess nudged his shoulder with her foot. It was time to for him to play spokesperson, so it didn't hurt so much when Hugh didn't recognize her.

Keeping quiet was better anyway. Opening her mouth with no sleep, no keys, and no breakfast was risking a public meltdown. She had to stay alert. Queen Ash could arrive at any moment.

Nero opened his eyes, blinked, and yawned, stretching out his arms. The princess jumped back to give him more room. Yawning was dangerous now that she had her own blackflies. She tried not to catch the yawn from Nero.

"Morning." Nero got up as if he hadn't spent the night on a bed of sharp tiny rocks. That answered her question about Blackfly beds. On top of everything else, her family probably wasn't getting enough sleep.

"It's looked better." He pointed at the castle. "No one will want to move in with the roof like that."

The princess gritted her teeth. "Our . . . *uh*, the Palace Agricultural Librarian is probably in there. If I get him to the window, could you explain we're here, *uh*, to fix the damage? Or King Schwartz sent us?"

"Queen Ash did," Nero said.

The princess coughed. "I wouldn't mention that."

Nero said nothing, and the princess wondered how close the Blackfly family was. Nobody liked to hear bad things about their own family.

Then he pointed up at the Tower. "How are you going to get his attention? Even if we yell, he won't hear us."

"Do you still have that black handkerchief?" the princess asked.

He handed it over, without asking what she wanted it for. Work was easier when people didn't expect you to explain. The princess rummaged through her pockets and found a clean but crumpled, silver one of her own, a threaded needle, a pencil, and a piece of paper. She stitched the two handkerchiefs together to make a tiny, silk balloon. This would have been a lot easier in her dungeon workshop.

At least the garden had a lot of new growth so it was easy

to find some bendable woody shoots. The new blackberry hedge didn't have Snow White proportions, but it tried to snag the princess's ankles a few times while she was cutting shoots from a non-thorny bush. She wove a crude little basket with a hoop on top that she planned to fit into the silk balloon. It had to be big enough so Hugh wouldn't mistake it for a rook flying by and ignore it.

Nero made approving noises and picked up the pencil and paper. "Do you want me to write while you do that?"

The princess hesitated. Hugh would probably recognize her handwriting, but as soon as he looked at her that wouldn't make any difference. Fiddling with sticks and stitching up handkerchiefs had taken up most of the morning. She nodded. "Just ask him to come to the window so we can talk to him."

Nero's pencil moved over the paper, and from the sound, wrapped up with a flourish. A Blackfly signature must be splashy.

The last thing the princess needed to work out was how to get the tiny balloon and basket up to the Tower. It wasn't a balloon—she didn't have a burner to make the hot air it needed to rise. But she could use the cable ferry idea to pull it up there, if she had a cable attached to the Tower.

Of course! The arrows from the christening. "I'll be right back," she told Nero and sped around to the vestibule where the archers stored their bows and arrows. A Blackfly disguise wouldn't help for this errand. She had to go alone.

The door to the archer's vestibule was open, and the archers were outside on a wooden bench, sipping peppermint tea and eating open-faced sandwiches. So far, so good.

TROUBLE WITH PARSNIPS

"Good morning," the princess called out as soon as her disguise turned her into a page. The lawn chairs meant the head archer wasn't there. That made everything easier. Inside the vestibule, a stone vase held the cabling arrows and the bows were hung on pegs. The princess took the smallest archer's bow and one arrow and went out.

The archers were too happy in the sunshine after the ordeals of the christening. No one questioned her even when she helped herself to two cheese sandwiches. The princess didn't blame them. They would need all their strength when Queen Ash arrived.

By the time the princess got back to Nero, he had finished his message and was fastening it into the basket so it wouldn't fly out. "Way to forage among the natives," he said, when he saw the sandwiches.

"Nice work yourself." The princess threaded the cable through the arrow's base, folded it exactly in half, nocked the arrow onto the bow, and aimed just above Hugh's window.

Twang!

The arrow flew up, up, up to the Tower and embedded itself into a beam over the window.

Thunk!

"Great shot!"

The princess tied the basket firmly onto the cable and held it up as high as she could, handing the free end of the cable to Nero. "Can you pull it up?"

Nero whipped leather gloves out of his pockets, put them on, and pulled the basket up with a will. He made the end fast by wrapping the extra cable around a boulder and tucking the end underneath. None of the Harolds could

Speaking Clearly with Tact Is an Art

have done it better.

"Perfect!" The sun was right overhead. The princess shaded her eyes and admired the tiny balloon bumping against Hugh's window. Now all they had to do was wait.

Nero grinned. "As soon as I get home, I'm getting some of those."

Oh well. If the Blackflies had their own cable arrows, the princess would just have to invent another way to defeat Queen Ash's archers.

"Ho there!" the Fire Chief barreled around the end of the castle with ten Cochem archers following. "I knew you were dangerous characters. Stand well back, archers, and bring them to the dungeon. Blackfly royals shooting arrows at Cochem Castle, inside and out. What are the Seven Kingdoms coming to?"

Nocking their bows, the archers formed a lethal arrow point aimed at Nero and the princess.

Hmm. This was not the way the princess had planned to use her Blackfly princess disguise. The archers were keeping their distance, so she couldn't turn into a page.

"Sorry about this," she said to Nero.

He shrugged. "We were shooting at the castle. They were bound to notice."

"Well done, archers! I'll just go, *umph*, secure the kitchen." The Fire Chief hiked his heavy belt up a little higher and walked off towards the castle.

Surrounded by bristling archers, The princess and Nero walked across the grass. If they hadn't been on their way to the dungeons, it would have been a perfect day for a picnic. White, puffy clouds drifted in the sky. The air smelled freshly washed.

The princess didn't have high hopes that Hugh would look out his window any time soon. At least they'd sent the message first.

"What kind of a dungeon do they have, you know, here?" Nero tilted his head to one side, and his eyes held a deeper question.

"Worried about getting out?"

"No." Nero's smile vanished. "I was thinking you might know a little too much about it."

She smothered a laugh. He seemed to think she needed rescuing.

"The Dungeon. Is. My. Workshop." She bored into his stubborn brown eyes with her own. "I was never a prisoner in Cochem's dungeon. Well, at least not until today. All seven of my, *um*, brothers, can break out of the workshop in five minutes." Her sisters did it in three. She'd taught them herself.

"Seven brothers?"

The princess sighed. Here it came. Put seven and seven and the princess together and you got Fifteenth. Then he would know they were on opposite sides too.

But Nero said, "No wonder you felt at home in Cochem. And all your brothers came over and tried out the dungeon. I guess the Blackfly Kingdom was too far." He sort of shook himself.

It must be tough living in a kingdom no one visited. Croquet fever wasn't a visit.

Glancing at the archers, Nero lowered his voice. "If getting out of the dungeon is a point of honor, I'm glad to have my turn."

Oops. The Blackfly crown prince probably told his mom

everything. Time to change the subject. "So tell me about the Blackfly dungeon. Do we have one?"

"Ours is better." He fell into step beside her. "We have this thing where you have to balance your feet on a paddle suspended over the water. It's so cool." He stood with his arms stretched out for balance, and then he shivered. His arms dropped, and he went on. "Unless you're in there too long, and then it's cold. Makes it hard to hit a croquet ball."

Queen Ash would take advantage of that. The princess had a vivid image of King Oliver holding onto a shivering Queen Sibyl. And then she wondered what Nero had done to land in his own dungeon. He couldn't have been in actual trouble.

"You forgot to take out the trash?" the princess guessed, raising her eyebrows.

Nero shook his head. "I won three matches of croquet in a row."

The princess had to be sure. "Against Queen Ash?"

"Yep." His face closed.

She winced. That was all the princess needed to know about the Blackfly dungeon. Before Queen Ash decided it needed more use, the princess wanted the Cochem family back home.

"Queen Ash says Blackfly Island is a natural place for prisoners. The blackflies are so much worse—" Nero described blackflies in a totally conversational tone until the princess felt things crawling down her neck and scratched her head with both hands.

If he was trying to keep her from asking personal questions, it was working.

TROUBLE WITH PARSNIPS

King Oliver had only forbidden locking people into the dungeon. He'd said nothing about locking visiting princes out. The princess had no trouble getting in or out herself, but she didn't want to tell a family secret like that to a Blackfly. Queen Ash would get it out of him in no time.

That meant she had to get to her workshop before Nero did. Galloping down the dungeon steps, she widened the gap between them, while wondering what her magical disguise would do with the Dungeon Master.

The Dungeon Master had no assistant because his daughter, Bridget, helped out when she wasn't washing dishes. *Hiding in plain sight* couldn't help the princess here. Most people remembered how many children they had.

Jumping over the crumbly third-step-from-the-bottom, the princess stepped into the dungeon antechamber, breathless.

"Speaking clearly with tact is an art," Bridget's voice echoed against the stone walls, and one arm extended gracefully towards an imaginary audience. Her scullery maid uniform didn't quite go with the gesture. Seeing the princess, Bridget dropped the pose. "Where have YOU been? I washed all the dishes by myself."

Also in her scullery maid outfit, the princess gave a little wave and kept right on down the tunnel to her workshop. She fumbled in her pocket. As soon as Nero and the archers caught up, her disguise would mess everything up. She had to hurry.

"Hey—come back here!" Bridget started after her, and the princess broke into a run.

A clatter of footsteps behind them meant the archers and Nero had reached the bottom of the stairs.

Speaking Clearly with Tact Is an Art

Bridget shouted, "Where do you think you're going? That's Fifteenth's workshop."

The princess didn't think she could bear it if this disguise took her workshop from her. Then she realized the Dungeon Master and Bridget must have kept all seven Harolds out of her workshop. That must be why no tools were lost last year. When King Oliver and Queen Sibyl came back, she'd have to arrange for a Medal of Honor.

She ran to the workshop's door, took the properly prepared paperclip out of her pocket, and stuck it in the almost invisible reset hole on the lock. *Click.*

Swinging the door open, she slipped inside and yanked to shut it after her, but Bridget stuck her foot in the gap.

They stood on each side of the door, pulling the door back and forth.

"Where did you get the key?" Bridget jerked her head towards the lock.

The princess couldn't answer and was out of breath. Once she got the heavy duty chain from under the workbench, she could secure the door with a big chain X. That would keep Bridget out.

The princess yanked on the door. Nero would come down the dungeon passage any moment. When he did, she didn't want to *hide in plain sight*, she wanted to be under her workbench, out of sight. Let him think there was a secret passage after all. If Bridget hadn't been practicing speeches in the dungeon, this would have worked. "Could. You. Please. Let go. Of the door. So I can lock myself. In my own dungeon?"

"It isn't your Dungeon," Bridget said. "My father is Dungeon Master here."

"Well, my father is king here," the princess said, without thinking.

"Right. Princess Soapsuds. I forgot." Bridget forced the door open and held out her hand. "Now give me that key or I'll get my father."

Hoping there was another paperclip in the workshop somewhere, the princess reached out and dropped the one she'd just used into Bridget's open palm. A pity. The princess kept the workshop paperclip-free, in case she needed to park a sibling there while she finished wrapping their birthday present.

Bridget shut the door with a clang and lit the wall torches.

At that moment, Nero stepped forward into the light with the archers all bunched up behind him. "Blackfly prisoners for you, ma'am," the first archer said.

When the Dungeon Master wasn't there, Bridget was second-in-command, but she didn't react. She was staring down at her open palm. "A paperclip? How did you know?"

The archer cleared his throat. Bridget's hand shut and she looked up, her jaw dropping when she saw the princess.

The princess shrugged. The disguise felt like a mean trick.

Bridget's forehead wrinkled. "So you turn it on and off? You think: 'Today, I'll be a scullery maid' and flip the switch. Royal people playing practical jokes. Because they don't have enough to do."

Nero's eyes flashed, and he folded his arms across his chest. "You will treat my cousin with respect, no matter what she is wearing."

Poor Bridget. The princess couldn't defend her by

Speaking Clearly with Tact Is an Art

showing Nero how the magic worked. Kizzy's gift seemed to prefer royalty to scullery maids.

The first archer coughed. "Excuse me, ma'am, but we're supposed to see these dangerous prisoners into the dungeon."

When Bridget didn't move, he added, "They were shooting arrows at the Tower."

"Were they now?" Bridget glared at the princess. "I don't know how a Blackfly Princess or a scullery maid got the . . . 'key.' No offense, but no one's allowed in there but the Fifteenth. Not even the other Cochem royals, unless she takes them in."

"*Uh*." The princess wished Bridget could see her as she was. This magical disguise needed an off switch. "I demand to speak to, *uh* . . ." A lawyer wouldn't help her. "To the PAL librarian!"

Nero's mouth pursed in split-second approval but his face smoothed as Bridget turned to him. He said, "So do I."

"*Uh*, no, you don't." The princess needed to talk to Hugh about castle defenses. Nero would be in the way. "It's your turn to, *uh*, you know."

"My turn?" Nero asked.

Willing him to remember her earlier story about her siblings, the princess tipped her head towards the locked workshop and mouthed, "point of honor."

"Oh! Right. Yes." Nero put his hands together and turned to Bridget. "I need to stay in the dungeon, I'm too . . . just ask the Fire Chief. He saw me shoot at the castle."

Bridget looked from one to the other. "I don't know what you people think you're doing, but I told you—no one goes in Fifteenth's workshop without her say so."

"*Uh*, can I talk to you for a moment?" The princess pointed down the tunnel. "Please? I helped you wash the dishes."

Nero made a disapproving sound but Bridget silenced him with a look. "Archers—keep a close eye on this prisoner." She took the princess down the tunnel. "That's far enough."

The princess's dress was still black. "Just a little more—" The tunnel curved, they left the others behind, and her apron showed up.

"Not again." Bridget rolled her eyes. "Would you make up your mind?"

"Sorry, I, *uh*, can't. I—turn into a Blackfly when he's near me." It wasn't Nero's fault, but it was true, in a way. Words were tricky that way.

"He's using *magic* to make you into a Blackfly?" Bridget scowled in Nero's direction, even though the tunnel's curve hid the others. "I knew the Blackflys were bad, but attacking scullery maids is the worst thing I ever heard."

The princess felt a little guilty blaming Nero. But what else could she do? She had to see Hugh alone, and she couldn't prove she was Fifteenth. Her only chance was using *hiding in plain sight* in whatever way she could.

"Leaving him in Fifteenth's workshop isn't right, but it's the only dungeon we have. I hope she'll understand." Bridget let out a long breath. "Okay. I'll take you up to the PAL. But then I'm getting the Dungeon Master. This is getting complicated."

When the princess and Bridget went back, Nero stood in the middle of the tunnel with his hands up. Archers surrounded him with bows and nocked arrows.

"Good work, archers," Bridget said and the princess felt even guiltier.

Taking out her keys, Bridget unlocked the princess's workshop, and the archers escorted Nero inside.

The princess couldn't meet his eyes. Without a paperclip, he'd be locked in. All she could do was get him out again as soon as possible and hope Queen Ash never found out.

The princess shivered. Explaining to King Oliver why she'd risked an InterKingdom Incident was going to be hard enough.

CHAPTER NINE
The Rook Egg

THE PRINCESS, BRIDGET, and a pair of Cochem archers, came out of the dungeon into low, slanting sunshine. The day was almost over, and the princess hadn't gotten anything done. She had to get Hugh to give her his keys and set Bridget straight so they could lock up as many of the castle's treasures as possible before Queen Ash arrived.

Even while crossing the lawn and climbing the spiral stairs to the Palace Agricultural Library, the princess's eyes fell shut again and again. It had been a while since she'd really slept, and no bed was in her immediate future.

The Palace Agricultural Library was on the top floor of the Tower, above the Hall, and right under the carrier pigeons. When they stepped inside, the princess caught her breath.

Wallpaper hung ragged from the walls and, on one wall, the bookcases were charred black. Broken glass lay on the Indian carpets. Sunlight poured in through the sashless windows. Hugh's was the only library chair that wasn't a heap of tattered leather and metal springs. The firefighters had been thorough with their axes.

The Rook Egg

"Ohhhhh." The poor PAL. The carpet stank of wet fireplace. She covered her mouth and nose with her hands. These books had rescued the kingdom from every possible danger.

"Lucky for you, the dungeon has dry beds. The rest of the castle is in terrible shape." Bridget walked from one set of bookcases to another, looking down the aisles, and, unfortunately, never going out of the princess's sight. "Where's Hugh?"

Hugh? The princess didn't know Bridget was on a first name basis with the PAL librarian. This whole new look at castle life was interesting, but the princess wished Bridget would look on the other side of the PAL, maybe in the picture books.

The door to Hugh's office was open, but he wasn't in. He always carried the keys to the rare bookshelves, but his other castle keys hung on their usual hook. The princess shot a quick glance at the archers and reached out to take the keys.

Bridget came around the corner of the bookshelf. The princess had to point at Hugh's desk and try to look innocent. "Hugh's not in here."

"I think I knew that." Bridget gave the princess a hard look and shut the office door. The princess would have to try again later. In the meantime, she would help the PAL.

Open books covered the long tables, and pages rustled in the breeze from the PAL's open windows. That meant Hugh was okay. Wherever he was at the moment, he'd already gotten started drying out the books.

How were they going to get all of this dry, repaired, and secure before Queen Ash showed up? This was a major wrinkle. More than once, Queen Ash had told King Oliver to send all those dusty PAL books up two rivers to the Frankfurt Book Fair. If she saw the PAL like this, she'd dump Cochem's most valuable treasures straight into the recycling.

The princess emptied the next bookcase onto the tables, ruffling the pages of the other books on each trip back to the bookcase. Bridget gave her an approving nod, but the princess felt guiltier with every trip. None of this would have happened, if she hadn't been trying for a name.

The cost for her name might be too high, not just for her, but for the whole kingdom. The princess wavered. Was it time to stop? A sagging strip of wallpaper caught her in the forehead, and she reached up and peeled it off the wall. Dropping it into the wastepaper basket, she forced the question out of her mind.

One crisis at a time. Whether she got a name or not, the PAL needed her. The wet books and carpets had to be dried so they could be locked up out of harm's way.

The new wallpaper could go right over the entrance. Queen Ash might never find her way in. Good thing Nero wasn't here. He couldn't tell Queen Ash what he didn't know.

That meant the PAL had to be cleared away before he got out. The princess dragged the wooden bookcase away from the wall to get at the next section of ruined wallpaper. It all had to come down before the new paper could go up.

At that moment, Hugh walked in with a stack of books, reading the one on top, his bushy gray hair sticking out in all directions.

The princess, in her scullery maid's uniform, went to him

The Rook Egg

but didn't know what to say first, especially with Bridget standing right there. "Uh–"

Other than a missing sweater button and a smudge of soot on his forehead, Hugh looked the same as always—as if someone had woken him up from a book. He glowered at the archers and pointed at the door. "We can dispense with armed individuals in the library."

The archers sidled out of the PAL.

Bridget pointed at the princess. "She's supposed to be in the dungeon, but she asked to speak to you instead of a lawyer. I have to find the Dungeon Master but prisoners can't be wandering all over the castle. Can you keep an eye on her until I get back?"

"Prisoner?" Hugh looked the princess up and down. "She's no prisoner. She practically lives in the dungeon, but she's a Cochem princess."

"Blackfly–" said Bridget.

"Cochem." Hugh's tone was so definite that the princess tugged on her apron to make sure it was real. It was. He'd recognized her anyway. The princess looked down at the soggy carpet, and a smile played around her mouth. The important thing was to find out how he'd done it.

Bridget didn't leave any room for the princess to ask. "She's definitely not a Cochem princess. She doesn't look like any of them, and she won't tell me her name. She's either a Blackfly princess . . ." Bridget's palm faced up and then down. "Or she's a scullery maid. If you can't keep her secure in the PAL, I'll have to take her back down to the dungeon."

The princess couldn't slip away. She needed Hugh's keys, and the most valuable treasures in Cochem were right here in the PAL.

"The archers said the two of them were attacking the castle." Bridget pulled back an imaginary bow and arrow and aimed at the window gap. Her fingers flicked against her thumb like the twang of the release. Bridget's imitation was so good, the princess caught herself following the flight of the imaginary arrow.

Hugh's eyes held an alarming gleam. "She didn't attack the castle. She sent me a message. If you want to keep the Blackfly prince in the dungeons, be my guest. But this one needs speech lessons. She never learned to speak up for herself."

If the princess preferred the dungeon, but no one asked her.

"No need for bows and arrows if you can speak up for yourself." Bridget shook her head, wisely. "Clear speaking is so important."

Hugh visibly calmed down. "I'm sure we can fit in a few lessons. In fact, she should fill out her Entry Form right away. This mess can wait that long."

Entry Form!? Queen Ash had forced Cochem to have a Speech Tournament, but no one could force the princess to speak in it.

"Shamefully. Neglected." Hugh's whiskery eyebrows came together, and he sank down into his splintery chair.

"No, never neglected," the princess put in quickly. "And especially not by you."

"Flatterer." Hugh smiled, but his eyes said he wasn't going to let it go. When he looked at her like that, it was best to get out of sight until he forgot about it. The princess moved behind a towering pile of damp books. She might as well

The Rook Egg

keep going with the book rescue. Nothing she could say would change Hugh's mind. He had to get it out of his system.

The princess fanned out the damp pages of each book, standing them up book after book on the longest table in the PAL, like triangular soldiers in a long line.

"I know." Bridget went eagerly over to Hugh's chair. "What she needs is the Vintner's Ventriloquism League—"

"Ventriloquists!" Hugh jumped up, the princess flinched, and Bridget took a step backward. "People need to know she's speaking to them!"

Honestly. The princess had to stop this. Hugh was going to keel over, and they'd have to take him to the hospital. She stuck her head around the books. "Please don't get excited—I'm not interested in the what's-it League. We already know speech lessons are pointless for me."

"Usually if you're bad at something, it only means you need a little more help." Bridget's head tilted to one side, and she smiled brightly at the princess, clearly on some kind of crusade. "The VVL is a friendly place to try something new. You'll love it. Oh—and if you join, you'll be my tenth new member. I'll get my Membership ribbon!"

When Hugh had first given the princess lessons, she'd really tried. But she never seemed to get any better, and she'd finally told him, "The PAL is so much more important. You're wasting your time with me. I just don't *get* speeches. Besides, I'll never have to give one—I have fourteen older brothers and sisters."

But Hugh hadn't given up. Finally, she'd stopped doing her homework. It had seemed kinder than wasting his time and driving up his blood pressure, but it was the one sore spot between them. The princess was more than a little annoyed at Bridget for stirring him up.

"The Tournament seems like a good time to start again," Bridget said.

"*Uh*, no it doesn't!" The princess should have seen this coming as soon as Queen Ash challenged Cochem to the Duel of the Halls.

Hugh sighed. "This can't go on like this. Maybe I've been too hasty in the past about the VVL . . ." After a moment, he gave Bridget a tiny bow. "I'll help as much as I can."

The princess's mouth dropped open. She'd never felt outnumbered in front of Hugh before. Her hands kept fanning out books, because they needed drying, but her insides felt all whizzy and whirry.

"Perfect." Bridget smiled. "If she comes to the VVL tomorrow night, she'll be ready in time for the Tournament."

"What?" Outnumbered or not, the princess was not going to be forced into the InterKingdom Speech Tournament. She called out from behind her fortress of books. "But if I'm really a Blackfly princess, your League won't take me."

Bridget shot back. "The VVL takes everyone. And once we're through with you, you can start a new club in the Blackfly Kingdom. Just imagine what would happen if Queen Ash joined. It's all about spreading the word."

The fervent light in Bridget's eye hinted at more ribbons to win. Speech-y people were nothing but trouble.

Of course, Hugh was nodding. Bridget was playing his favorite song.

"I'll get started with the princess right away." He waved a book at the princess but he was looking at Bridget. "She'll

The Rook Egg

need all the time we have to prepare, if she's going to give a winning speech."

Bridget thanked him and went out. The door of the PAL closed behind her, and the princess was alone with Hugh and the ravaged library. Her apron vanished, and a grubby cardigan sweater appeared.

"Trust me," Hugh said. "You need this Tournament. I'll teach you everything I know. You've got a decent chance at making your parents hear you."

The princess couldn't learn to give a speech. She'd tried. She held up her hands with her fingers splayed out like a frustrated police officer. Weren't 14 trophies enough for Hugh?

He couldn't teach her anything that would make her family pay attention. They all had croquet fever, and the princess had to defend the castle until they got here. She went to the door of his office. She needed his keys, not another project. "There's no time—"

"I didn't realize I was missing a button." Hugh pointed at her cardigan's gaping buttonhole and the matching one on his own.

The princess stopped short. Hugh knew her disguise copied the person next to her. Was that how he'd recognized her?

"If you have a fairy godmother's gift, you have a name."

The princess coughed. "Uh, no."

"All this?" Hugh waved an arm at the spoiled PAL. "And still no name?"

The princess didn't want to talk about it. "Queen Ash has the Golden Parsnip."

Hugh made considering noises so the princess waited.

You had to give librarians time to update their systems before you asked to borrow their keys.

After a moment, Hugh said, "Now that I think of it, there are some gifts . . . you don't happen to remember what your gift is called?"

She told him. Almost before the words were out of her mouth, he dashed into his office. She followed, but he kept looking over his shoulder at her so she had no chance at the keys. The hinges of his desk creaked, and the glass panels of the rare book shelf shuddered.

"Look at this." Hugh came over to her with a tiny book open on his palm. "Is this the gift the foolish creature gave you?" His big stubby finger covered half the page. He handed the princess his magnifying glass. They went into the other part of the PAL, where the light was better.

"*Hiding in plain sight*" was written across the top.

"Why can we see it?" Unless a fairy held the book, the print was invisible.

Hugh shook his head absently. "I had a copy made."

Cochem's PAL librarian had copied a fairy book. The princess's world shifted. No wonder he kept it locked up. This must be the only copy in the Seven Kingdoms.

"But this is your gift? You're sure?" The worry in his voice made her feel worse.

"Is it so bad?" The disguise would have been better with an off switch, but it wasn't terrible.

With an even stronger lens and a bright lamp, Hugh was studying the tiny print that Kizzy hadn't been able to read in her Nectar-stained book.

Hugh grunted, held his place with tweezers, and asked the princess to bring him a fairy language dictionary with a

The Rook Egg

green binding from the bottom shelf. That was more like Hugh.

She got the short, fat book and handed it to him, but he didn't take it.

"Look up wild-type for me."

She sat on the wet, smoky carpet, and opened it on her lap. Hugh didn't make any comment.

When she found the entry and showed him the fairy word, shimmering on the page, he frowned. "It's just what I thought. That silly fairy gave you a gift that still has a very active wild-type."

"What's a wild-type?" the princess asked.

"You might be in a bit of trouble." He gave her a testing look. "Are you positive you don't have a name?"

Usually Hugh believed her, even when no one else did. She glared at him. "If I had one, I would've signed up for a library card."

Hugh grunted. Then his eyebrows came together again. "How long would it take to get another christening set up?"

The princess hadn't had time to think about that yet. "It took six months to find a day when all Seven Kingdoms were available, and I don't know how long it takes to get the Bishop."

"You don't have six months." Hugh rifled through the pages in his desk calendar until he got to today's date. "One, two, three, four, five days since the christening party didn't happen. That leaves 10 days for you to get it organized before the wild-type kicks in. You've got to have the new christening by the 15th, at the latest."

10 days. The princess rubbed her ears. She couldn't have heard that right, and he still hadn't told her what the wild-

type was. She also had a vague sort of niggling feeling about the 15th, but she couldn't drag her thoughts away from that terrible 10 days to think about it properly. "But what is the wild-type?"

"Kizzy is going to end up in front of the examination board." He held out the fairy book copy and the lens to her. "See this word? It means 'wild-type' in faerie. If you don't have a name, your magical disguise goes back to its wild type. You'll be invisible for the rest of your life."

Leaving the princess frozen to the spot, he clapped the book shut and got her a pile of carrier pigeon message slips and a pen.

The princess took them but she couldn't take in what he'd said. Invisible. Without a name. Her family would really forget she existed. That sounded worse than being dead.

Being invisible would make defending the castle even harder. She sat down at a library table and wrote:

King Oliver and Queen Sibyl request the honor of your presence at a Royal Christening for the Fifteenth Child of the Kingdom of Cochem on the 15th Day of...

At first, the motion of the pen helped her think. This time, she was sending the Bishop's invitation first. Hugh told her the Bishop was a serious birder, so the princess added a note about the Cochem rooks. It couldn't hurt.

The royal address book was fat, and the princess's eyes and hand ached before she was half-way through. The date sounded so familiar. She rested her forehead on her fist for a moment while she tried to remember what else could be happening on the 15th. Nothing came to her. Her brain was only playing tricks because she'd written 15th so many

The Rook Egg

times.

ea·ea·ea

A crinkle of invitation paper under her cheek woke the princess. The PAL's windows were bright with moonlight, and Hugh was gone. The princess got a lamp, and helped herself to the keys. Then she hunted for him. Sending out the invitations by carrier pigeon would be much easier with two people.

Hugh could be anywhere even though it was the middle of the night. The princess rushed back through the history section to the ancient Romans and found an open book about Abyssinian art next to his second-favorite armchair. Hugh wasn't in his armchair, but something else was.

A bundle of twigs?

Ohhh. The princess peeked inside. The pearly, green speckled surface of the rook egg shone in the moonlight. It was a nest. She stroked the surface of the egg with one careful finger, and her heart leapt up.

Actually, the princess hadn't seen any signs of rooks since the fire. Smoke or water or both must have driven them all away. All but the one rook egg.

A Cochem rook was as valuable as a rare book. The princess had to keep it safe from Queen Ash, who would take it back to the Blackfly Kingdom when she left or decide that black rooks were a sign she should live in Cochem permanently.

The princess scooped up the egg, nest and all, and put it into her pocket. After all, the hole in the ceiling meant the nest had fallen down from the parapet. It didn't belong to the PAL. As long as she saw the rook's shiny black eyes first, Hugh could demand whatever library fine he liked. It would be magic to have a wild rook come when she called. She could teach it to listen to her. To know her voice.

Unless she really turned invisible. She stuck out her lip and pushed the thought away. Invisible people shouldn't have to pay library fines anyway, so there.

A flash of white caught her eye, and she picked up something that had been hidden underneath the nest. It was a note from Hugh.

To: *The youngest and brightest inventor princess of Cochem*

Dear Fifteenth,

I've been unexpectedly called away on urgent library business. I know you will do all you can to look after <u>this</u> *and the PAL while I'm away. I'll look in on your parents and try to bring them back in time.*

Best regards,

Hugh Ancry

Palace Agricultural Librarian

Cochem Kingdom

Huh. The princess couldn't imagine what urgent library business would make Hugh leave the PAL in this state. He also didn't notice time passing. She had little hope of him bringing her parents home any earlier.

She went back to her table and collected the tiny invitations. The pigeons did the flying, but loading them up without Hugh's help would take hours.

Out in the stairwell, she lifted the heavy wooden Palace Agricultural Library sign off its hooks next to the door and dragged it inside under the nearest table. Leaving the windows open, she went out again, locking the door behind

The Rook Egg

her. If Queen Ash showed up, maybe she would mistake the unmarked door for something else.

Actually, that wasn't a bad idea. The princess ran down the stairs, swiped the sign from the broom closet, and hung it up outside the PAL.

It wasn't much, but she couldn't do more right now. Once the invitations were out and the rook egg was under a warm brooder lamp in her workshop, then she would get the PAL dry and well-defended.

CHAPTER TEN
Brooding in the Dungeon

IN THE VERY top of the castle's Tower—one flight up from the Palace Agricultural Library—the dovecote housed Cochem's carrier pigeons. The entrance on the parapet was convenient for bird, man, and girl. Before the princess went in, she looked for any sign of her family.

One side of the valley was in shadow, and the other was all bright green leaves. In between, the Mosel River reflected the kingdom on its dark liquid surface. No Cochem silver was visible in any direction.

The princess went into the dovecote and got to work. Catching carrier pigeons, loading their leg tubes with fifteen hundred invitations, and releasing them took her the rest of the morning.

As she got hungrier, she got slower, and the pigeons got craftier. Seven Kingdoms' worth of invitations and no guarantee anyone would accept. If Hugh hadn't had an emergency cookie jar up here, she would have starved before she'd sent off even half.

When the last carrier pigeon took to the air, the princess headed down through the castle, longingly sniffed the good

Brooding in the Dungeon

scents of the kitchen, cut across the garden, and let herself into the dungeon tower.

According to Hugh, the princess only had nine more days of visibility, ten counting today. She unlocked the door to her workshop, planning to get the brooder lamp, set it up somewhere it wouldn't be noticed, and get right back to work in the PAL.

Oops. Nero was comfortably reading in a big armchair in the middle of the princess's workshop. If he hadn't escaped, why hadn't Bridget thrown him out?

The princess stepped into the cell. Behind her, the door fell shut and locked.

"You're back." He closed his book—a brand new one on rooks she'd requested from Hugh—and laid it on a small table.

Wait, he had . . . *furniture?*

A floor lamp stood conveniently next to Nero's armchair. His bare feet rested on a Persian rug with deep, cushy pile. The bed against the side wall was covered in silver brocade and fluffy pillows. He didn't look like he would be filing an InterKingdom complaint.

"Uh, you're still here."

He winced. "I was taking a break before I tried again. You know, a fresh attack."

She gritted her teeth, glancing around the cell.

No tools littered a workbench that wasn't there. No hot air balloon or cable ferry parts filled the missing shelves or hung on a wall suddenly without hooks. She was having a nightmare. "Who, *uh*, redecorated?"

"The Dungeon Master, maybe? I was out in the rain for all of it, so I don't really know." Nero smiled at the floor and rubbed the back of his neck. "I helped carry the bed in when the stonemasons were finished."

"Stonemasons." The whole dungeon looked . . . smaller and square-ish as if the back wall had been moved in. She and Bridget had talked about doing it a year or so ago, when the Harolds kept swiping her best set of hex wrenches for a bicycle race. The princess had even drawn a sketch of a secret room.

"The Dungeon Master said a corner of the dungeon got damaged during that storm—you know, the night you were in that shelter." The princess nodded, and he went on, "Must have been lots of damage because it took almost all night to fix it. The rain last night didn't help."

Going to the wall, she laid a hand on a stone and pushed hard. It didn't budge. She ran her hand along the stones, and Nero coughed.

"I don't think you can get out that way. It's solid." He'd tested it too then.

The princess tried to act as if she wasn't still checking the wall, stone by stone. Her finger found a smooth brass keyhole in the rough stone. A secret keyhole meant a secret door meant at least a secret broom closet.

Right now, it was a perfect roadblock between the princess and the brooder lamp. But if no Blackfly knew about it, it could be a perfect defense against their upcoming invasion.

The princess had to find out what Nero knew. He seemed nice enough but Queen Ash was his mom. "You were in here with all the . . . dust?"

Nero shook his head. "I helped take the bed out, and I kind of leaned on it for a moment. The next thing I knew,

Brooding in the Dungeon

the Dungeon Master was waking me up so they could bring it in. Whatever they were doing in here was done."

Nero didn't know. The princess sagged against the wall. When King Oliver got back, the princess was going to suggest a Medal of Honor for the Dungeon Master. They'd built a fake wall in one night.

The bedspread wasn't black, but otherwise it looked like Nero was moving in permanently. "You didn't make a break for it ... in the garden?"

"It was a point of honor." Nero gave her a puzzled look as if she wasn't quite up to par as a princess.

She snatched up the book he'd been reading and opened it, even though she knew what she'd see on the first page—point of honor or not.

Yep. The stamp marked it as Palace Agricultural Library property. Blackflys didn't waste any time helping themselves to valuables. "Where did you get this?"

"I checked it out." Nero pulled out his wallet, took out a card and waggled it at her.

PALACE AGRICULTURAL LIBRARY

The princess was too busy looking through the stack of books on Nero's table. All the ones she'd begged Hugh to get for the PAL that were too expensive for a small kingdom. She took a deep breath.

"Are you okay?" Nero laid his library card on the table.

"If you didn't . . . *uh*, escape, how did you get these?" she whispered, gesturing at the books. Was he getting books out of the PAL while she was sleeping on a table? Her face burned.

Nero smiled. "Your Royal Librarian brought them by on his way out. He said they were in a brand new shipment, and he thought you might be interested. He's quite a guy."

The princess picked up the card and looked at the back for Hugh Ancry's signature. She gave the card back to Nero without a word. Nero hadn't seen her asleep in the PAL, but this was humiliating enough.

"What is it?" Nero asked. "Hugh said something about you getting one too, after the Tournament, but don't you already have one?"

"No." The princess didn't appreciate Hugh's methods. He'd probably thought she needed a reminder of what the Tournament could do for her—as if a speech could ever get her a name. So he'd given a card to a Blackfly.

"Hugh said you were in the PAL." Nero opened the brand new rook book. It already had a yellow REFERENCE sticker on the binding. "Why you didn't come down with him?"

The princess took a firm grip on her temper. She needed to get rid of Nero, and all prisoners needed exercise. "Did you get a walk yet?"

"I was in the garden all night and overslept this morning so I didn't even see who brought me lunch." Nero shut his book.

Rats. He wanted to chat, but if he couldn't escape, he had to read. "Does that book have anything about rook eggs?

Brooding in the Dungeon

Like, *uh*, how long they need to hatch?"

Nero's eyebrows went up, but he opened the book and hunted through the index, just as she'd hoped.

She went over to the brass keyhole, checked that he wasn't looking and tried the first key. *Nope.* One down, fourteen to go.

"Eggs, hatching..." Nero turned to the page. "14 to 21 days, somewhere between two and three weeks."

Maybe her family would be over their croquet fever by then, and the princess could enjoy the chick in peace.

"It says it depends how old the egg is," Nero said.

Desperate, the princess took it out of her pocket and held it up. "Five or six days, I think."

Nero whistled. Reluctantly, she let him take it. It would keep him busy looking things up in her book. He rumpled up the bedspread, laid the egg down in a soft, brocade nest, and went over to his wall calendar.

Whistling to cover the scrape of the keys, the princess tried out five more.

Nero counted days aloud. "Seven, eight, nine, ten, eleven, twelve, thirteen, fourteen..."

Trying out the next three keys, the princess stopped listening.

"Look–" Nero had one hand on the fourteenth and one on the twenty-first. "It has to hatch somewhere in here." He did a push-up against the wall and touched his chin to the fifteenth.

The 15th was the perfect day for the hatch and one more reason the christening had to work. If the chick didn't see you, it wouldn't talk to you.

"It would be great to have it hatch at the opening

ceremonies, wouldn't it?" Nero smiled at her.

The princess's jaw dropped. That was why the 15th had seemed so familiar while she was writing invitations. The InterKingdom Speech Tournament was on the Exact. Same. Day. Her christening was done for.

"Haven't you had any speech lessons?" Nero must have seen her look of horror. He took her elbow and parked her in his armchair.

"Yes and no," she answered automatically.

"What kinds of lessons did you take?" he asked.

"Just the usual. Limericks, villanelles, haikus."

"Limericks? You mean poems? Like sonnets?"

He got the definite feeling he was asking questions to make her feel better. She shook her head regretfully. "I can't do sonnets."

"Sonnets I can see, but limericks? What do you need those for? Limericks have nothing to do with statecraft." He seemed very sure of himself. Maybe he'd missed the lesson on the Poet-King.

"Did you spend a lot of time learning statecraft?" She swatted a blackfly. Pompousness seemed to bring them out. The Blackfly Kingdom would benefit from insect research.

But the long, dry explanation helped the princess get herself together again. Nero gazed nobly into the distance and described his statecraft lessons. They didn't sound very useful, but the princess had time to try out the rest of the keys.

"How about pets?" she asked in the middle of an explanation about diplomacy. The princess was blocking out the whole christening problem by imagining her brooder set-up in detail. "Do you have any? Cats? Dogs?"

Brooding in the Dungeon

Startled, he looked over at her, and she whisked the keys into her pocket. "We don't keep animals. Do you?"

Blackflies were too small to count. "You mean you don't have a horse or anything?"

He flinched. "When I was small, I had a pet leech."

"You had a . . . a leech?" The princess was sure diplomacy wouldn't be served by laughing. She bit her lip but couldn't keep her smile from leaking out on both sides. He'd had a challenging childhood.

He looked pained. "What's so funny? They're really quite elegant in the water. Stretchy was a truly noble pet."

"Stret-chy?" She sagged against the stone wall, helplessly smacking it with the flat of her hand. "Noble leech, I knight thee protector of my kingdom . . . but where are your shoulders so I can smite thee with the flat of my blade?"

"Very. Funny. If you'll excuse me, I have to take another crack at this dungeon now." Nero walked over to the door and inspected it, his hands on his hips as if brain power alone could open it.

Once Nero's back was turned, the princess checked the whole wall for a tiny hole that might be a paperclip reset, but whoever had built it had decided not to add one.

Chalk up another fail to Kizzy's christening gift.

Bridget had seen a Blackfly princess use a paperclip on the workshop door and probably figured it was a security leak. But the princess was positive Bridget had the key.

The princess was done here. She left her paperclip on the PAL books, and put the egg went back into her pocket. Walking around Nero, she unlocked his door.

"Noooo—this is so embarrassing." Nero covered his eyes. "Lock me in again."

TROUBLE WITH PARSNIPS

"If you insist." The princess shrugged. When she got back with the key, he was going out—no matter what. She didn't want an audience for the secret room.

⁂

From the sound of Bridget's voice in the hallway, the princess didn't have far to go. Bridget stopped practicing her speech in mid-sentence. "Wasn't Hugh keeping an eye on you?"

A princess was supposed to mind her manners, but she was hungry, tired, and all this explaining was getting on her nerves. "Do you have a key to the secret door?" Deep breath. "Or do I have to get it from the Dungeon Master?"

"How do—I mean, what secret door?" Bridget asked as if she hadn't already given herself away.

Bridget was a loyal subject of Cochem, maybe even a little too loyal. The princess took the egg out of her pocket and held it up. She spoke slowly and clearly because she was afraid she wouldn't get through the sentence any other way. "If I don't. Get the brooder lamp. Soon. This egg is going to. Die."

Bridget's eyes narrowed. "I don't want to be rude, but I don't think the Cochem Kingdom gives away rook eggs to visiting Blackfly princesses. Or scullery maids."

The princess wasn't either but she didn't try to prove it. Asking for help was easier if she stayed focused on the egg. She held out her hand. "Key?"

"Rook eggs only hatch for Cochem princesses—"

Everyone in Cochem knew that.

Bridget tapped her foot. "Or for rooks. But the egg can't tell me who you are before it's too late." Her head tilted to one side. "Playing with a brooder shouldn't do any harm, and it might keep the egg safe until a real Cochem princess shows up."

The princess waited. If you were patient, people sometimes told you what you wanted to know.

"Hugh vouched for you before he left." Bridget made *hmmm*-ing noises as if she were trying to decide something.

The princess hoped Bridget would say more about Hugh's urgent business.

"It's about time Hugh sees what the VVL can do." A broad smile filled Bridget's face but her tone was dead serious when she turned to the princess. "Okay. This is the plan—I'll take you into the workshop and set up that brooder on one condition."

"Fine." The princess didn't care what the condition was. She wanted that key. Without her workshop, she couldn't save this egg, fix the dessert sluice, take down soggy wallpaper in the PAL to keep the books from death by mold or do anything else she needed to do to defend the castle.

"I'll lock you into your workshop with the egg, and you can set up the brooder, if you come to the Vintner's Ventriloquism League tomorrow night and sign up for the Tournament." Bridget put her hands on her hips as if she expected the princess to argue.

Tomorrow and the Tournament were in the future, and the princess had tools to get out of any workshop. Maybe she could make do without the key. She shook Bridget's outstretched hand. "Done."

"Oooh—I can't wait to get my ribbon! Then I'll have one more than the Dungeon Master."

After that, it was easy. Bridget sent Nero out with the

archers for his required hour of exercise and unlocked the secret door.

The princess walked into her workshop and stopped dead. "Ah—Where are my tools?" She leaned on her empty workbench to hold herself up.

"The tools are in those boxes." Bridget pointed to a row of alphabetical wooden crates along the wall. "You tell me what you need, and I'll unlock it."

The Dungeon Master had built a room within a room—or had it built—so that her workshop wouldn't be invaded. The floor of the workshop shone with a fresh coat of wax. A bed with silver velvet hangings stood in one corner.

What an excellent use for parsnip crates! And what an excellent dungeon staff Cochem had! The princess breathed again, and a wonderful idea came to her. The Dungeon Master would be the perfect person to work on the castle defenses. The next time she saw him, she would ask him.

"Can't you just unlock them all?" the princess said. She'd feel better if her tools were free.

Bridget's eyes narrowed. "I'm letting you use Fifteenth's tools for one thing, not giving you free rein."

The princess couldn't argue with protecting Fifteenth's stuff, but it was a slow, painful game. She asked for the 'B' crate and found the brooder. "I'd like the L, O, and W."

She found the warming Lamp, and Oil to burn in it, the Waterer for the chick and the Wood shavings for soft bedding. Even so, it took a lot longer than she'd hoped. Then she guessed wrong five more times without finding anything that would keep the hatched chick from wandering away the warm lamp.

Bridget tapped her foot. "Time's up."

The princess tried to explain what she was looking for, by making a circle of her arms. "It's about this big."

"What about this chick corral?" Bridget opened the 'C' crate and pulled it out.

Not bad. At this rate, King Oliver would have to order a parsnip crate 'M' full of Medals of Honor.

"Thank you so much," the princess said and got to work putting it all together.

"You're welcome." Bridget locked up all of the crates and topped up the water in a vase of Black tulips.

"In case I really am a Blackfly?" The princess's spirits sank. The detail-oriented Dungeon Master wouldn't make a mistake like that for a Cochem princess. So he didn't know.

"It's not my job to know." Bridget shrugged. "You might be. You might not be. The Cochem Dungeon shows hospitality to everyone. That's what my father says." She went out, turning the key in the secret door.

Twenty minutes later, the Dungeon Master paid the princess a visit. She was crouching down next to the rook egg when her magical disguise promptly transformed her into a scullery maid. The princess felt she should have known.

He set a completely unexpected platter of sandwiches, fruit and cocoa on the table next to her bed.

"Ohhh, thank you!"

He gave her a little bow. "It's my job, ma'am. Dinner is at 8 and breakfast at 9. Lunch is at 12."

Food and a dry bed were the whipping cream on top. The rook egg under the brooder lamp was super-duper chocolate sauce. But more than anything, the princess enjoyed the feeling of having friends who stood up for Fifteenth. In a funny way, it meant they saw her even if they didn't recognize that she and Fifteenth were the same person.

"You'll find extra blankets in the chest over there." The Dungeon Master pointed to a familiar round-topped wooden chest where the princess normally kept her favorite tools. It had no letter and no lock.

Thinking about her hex wrench set got her ridiculously choked up, and the Dungeon Master was gone before she could ask him to take on the castle defenses. Not that she had any idea how a scullery maid could ask that question and get a serious answer.

※※※※

The princess slept well that night in her secret workshop and woke to the gentle glow of the brooder lamp and the knowledge that she was safe, dry, fed, and among friends. Unless Nero had finally escaped, he was probably next door in the regular dungeon.

When she got out of bed, she remembered the VVL meeting. She'd been so sure she could escape any dungeon, she'd promised to go.

The long day alone, without access to the tools in the alphabetized parsnip crates, gave her too much time to discover how secure her new workshop was. The only small window was reinforced with bars. When she'd left her last properly prepared paperclip with Nero, she hadn't known she'd be locked in another dungeon so soon. But a paperclip wouldn't have helped if she'd had one. No reset anywhere.

If the Cochem archers had taken the princess for regular exercise, she could have used *hiding in plain sight* to slip away as a lowly page. No one ever looked at pages. But Bridget watched the princess much too closely, and Nero's cell was always empty when they went through it. Either he had finally escaped or he'd gone out for exercise with the Dungeon Master.

Whenever the rook egg was nestled in her hands, the princess could imagine surviving the Vintner's Ventriloquism League meeting. A rook chick was worth one evening of torture.

But an Entry Form was too much to ask of a nameless princess. She should have haggled more. Hour by hour, the VVL meeting grew in her mind into a deadly path leading to the Speech Tournament.

By afternoon, the princess was frantic. Yesterday, she'd thought it would be easy to escape, but this was a fortress not a workshop. The new stone wall was so thick she couldn't hear Nero if he was ever on the other side.

Whenever the princess managed to stop worrying about the VVL and the Tournament for a moment, she worried about her family. If they didn't get healthy soon, she was afraid they were all going to be homeless. It was hard to defend Cochem from the dungeon.

The Dungeon Master hadn't been by again, so the princess couldn't even ask him to help. Bridget said he was getting ready for the VVL meeting.

Argh! Speeches were as bad as croquet fever. The princess couldn't send a message. Bridget would tell her father the princess was nothing but a scullery maid under a Blackfly spell and had no business asking about castle defenses. The Dungeon Master might believe a written message, especially if he read it after the princess had died in battle.

When Bridget arrived with an almost-midnight-snack, the princess asked for paper to make a Will.

Bridget almost dropped her tray. "To make a what?"

"I have a rook chick to think of," the princess said.

"You have a—" Bridget gave a peal of laughter and banged the secret door with her palm a few times on the way out. "Oh, how am I going to get through my speech tonight without laughing?"

The princess didn't see what was so funny. If the VVL meeting didn't actually kill her, the Tournament would make her into a nameless voice. She wouldn't be able to tell her family where the kingdom's most valuable treasures were hidden. A Will made perfect sense.

"No, I won't bring you paper." Still laughing, Bridget shook her head. "No one has ever died from giving a speech."

CHAPTER ELEVEN

The Peppermint Tea House

At twenty minutes before midnight, the mist covered the river, drifting here and there into the village like sleepy clouds. In matching navy cloaks, the princess and Bridget came down through the vineyard on a long staircase, left the starry sky behind, and melted into the mist.

The princess didn't feel like talking. To save the rook egg, she'd promised to come to the Vintner's Ventriloquism League meeting, but she hadn't promised to stay. As soon as she got Bridget's secret room key, the princess was heading for the exit.

The Peppermint Tea House was in the middle of the village, right on a crowded square.

"But it's the middle of the night," the princess said, looking around at the vintners, parsnip farmers, milliners, and barge crews.

Bridget gave her a funny look. "There's a Tournament coming up, and this is the best place to practice giving speeches."

The princess gave a bitter laugh. She had no plans to make herself ridiculous by coming here more than once.

"How can you practice giving a speech? Either you can speechify or you can't."

"I'm guessing this is overdue," Bridget said, to no one in particular.

The princess ignored her. Her fourteen siblings also thought everyone should be speech-givers.

She and Bridget worked their way forward to the fountain in the square's center. A circle of lamps with colored lampshades threw rainbows over the shooting spray. She stopped to admire her design in action.

"Nice, isn't it?" Bridget came up next to her. "The VVLers light it every night there's a meeting."

If the VVLers liked her fountain, they couldn't be so bad, could they?

Then the princess remembered the two ventriloquists who had ignored her call for help. If they were anything like the rest... she was walking into a room full of people who had no use for the royal family. King Oliver should give them a thorough talking-to.

Then the thought that she might have to give anyone a talking-to made her hyperventilate. She bent down to put her head next to her knees.

Bridget pulled her upright and opened the massive wooden door of the mint-green building. "After you."

The hubbub continued into the Peppermint Tea House, but the princess took a deep breath and went in. She glanced down at her cloak to see how it had decided to blend in, but it was too dark to see.

A harmonica band was playing on stage but Bridget grabbed the princess's arm and shouted into her ear, "We're usually in the back room."

The princess focused on her duty to protect Cochem's treasures, thought of the tiny rook chick to come, and allowed herself to be led through a door into sudden quiet.

The back room was well-lit, with neat rows of round-back chairs, and a podium hung with a giant VVL insignia. Tilting her head, the princess read the writing that curved around it: The Vintner's Ventriloquism League.

She sat down in the nearest chair, afraid to look around. Trapped in the shelter, she had pictured sweeping into the VVL meeting with King Oliver, Queen Sibyl, and a dozen or more siblings to set the vintners straight on their shelter duty. Her family might ignore her, but in the middle of them all, she felt safe.

The room was filling now, and a woman in her row sounded like the one who had dismissed the fifteenth royal child as a prankster. The princess shifted uneasily in her seat.

Bridget came over with a name tag sticker, a pen, and a two-page agenda. She'd hung up her cloak, and her keys jingled cheerfully at her belt. The princess's fingers itched.

"Here, fill this out." Bridget handed the princess the "Hello, My Name is _____" sticker and the pen.

The princess hated these things. Fifteenth wouldn't work here. After a moment, she wrote "Twyla" in the blank. She might as well try out a name.

The princess put on the name tag and pocketed the paperclip from the agenda. Her gift seemed to have settled on a scullery maid outfit. Perfect. No one would ever know she'd been here.

"It's your first time, so you have to sit on the back bench." Bridget pointed at her name tag, "I knew it wasn't

Soapsuds."

"*Uh*, without you?" The air seemed thinner than normal. If the princess sat on the back bench with the ventriloquists and dummies, her disguise would change, and Bridget's key would be hopelessly out of reach.

The princess looked at her in mute appeal, but Bridget only pointed to the last empty spot on the back bench. "Reggie Giant is in charge of the meeting tonight," Bridget whispered in her ear, "he's the biggest parsnip farmer in Cochem."

The princess perched on the edge, ready to flee at a moment's notice. She was having trouble breathing.

"As soon as you say three sentences to the whole club, you can move up and sit with me. That's the definition of a speech." Bridget smiled, as if the princess would survive the experience.

"Three sentences is a speech?" Three sentences to this crowd was like hiking an ice-covered mountain peak in flip-flops.

Bridget gave her a sharp look. "You don't have to be smart-alecky about it. A real speech is almost always longer. It's a *minimum*. From the InterKingdom Tournament rules. People have to start somewhere you know."

The princess mumbled an apology for smart-alecky thoughts she'd never had. It was easier.

"Besides, think of King Oliver's great-great grandfather." Bridget wasn't letting it go. "It's *nevah, nevah, nevah too late for parsnips* isn't even three sentences." She left the princess and sat in the front row, right under the podium.

King Oliver the First's famous speech was actually quite a bit longer, but the princess wasn't going to argue. She sat down in the spot Bridget had indicated. Until she got the key, she couldn't make a run for it.

Hiding in plain sight considerately provided her with a ventriloquist's dummy in the form of a rook, as if it was reminding her what she was there for. She took a shaky breath. She hadn't studied statecraft, and speech lessons hadn't ever helped, but every royal child knew about fear.

It couldn't last forever, even when it felt that way. Closing her eyes, she pictured the rook egg in her hands for courage. She might be magically disguised for the rest of her life, but at least one living thing would recognize her first.

All around her, the other back benchers were yukking it up with their dummies. A roomful of speakers probably used up all the air in the room in no time. It wasn't safe.

The huge parsnip farmer approached the podium and banged on it with a gavel. "Welcome ReVVLers! Welcome guests! Let the meeting begin."

Everyone sat down, and the room fell silent.

"I'd like to ask the guests to introduce themselves—"

In the front row, Bridget swiveled around and gestured that the princess should stand up.

The princess shook her head.

Bridget got up and ran back to the princess, whose disguise promptly turned back into a scullery maid.

The whole row of interested ventriloquists turned towards the frozen "scullery maid." Bridget passed her hand back and forth in front of the princess's eyes. "Just say your name and that you came with me. It's not hard. Take a deep breath first, and look at everyone, and then talk."

Easy if you had a name. A deep breath was out of the

question, and the princess really, really didn't want to look around the room first, but she was the only Cochem princess at home, even if no one could tell. Considering what the VVL thought about royals, that was probably a good thing. She gritted her teeth and forced herself to stand up.

The back bench rustled, snickered, and let their dummies' wooden mouths clatter, but the rest of the room turned towards her, smiling.

"My naaaaame is . . ." Blanking out for a moment, she looked down at her name tag. "Twylaaaaa. I caaaaame with my friend. Thaaaaaank you." She sat down to the sound of clapping and whistling. Her chair felt reassuringly solid in a way that her knees didn't.

She'd never had a roomful of people clap for her before. It made her feel warm, even though her whole body was shaking.

"Quick!" Bridget yanked the princess by the arm and raced up to the front row under the podium. They sat down, panting for breath and Bridget's keys poked the princess's side.

Excellent. The princess had survived the worst. She just had to convince Bridget to give her the keys.

When the other guests were introduced, the princess clapped as hard as the others, trying to think of something to swap. If this kept up, her hands would be sore tomorrow morning.

Bridget nudged her and pointed out the program, written on the wall in colorful chalk. At the podium, Mr. Giant explained that four VVLers would be giving a speech.

He banged his gavel on the podium. "The first speech

tonight is: "Get'em while they're hot!" and our first speaker is our very own, Peter the parsnip auctioneer and his partner dummy, the parsnip farmer Pumpkineater—"

Everyone clapped again, and the princess joined in. All this terror had her wide awake. Clapping was easy.

Peter the parsnip auctioneer's speech about parsnip oven fries made the princess very hungry.

"Wow! That was amazing!" she shouted in Bridget's ear. "I wish I could give a speech like that."

Bridget kept clapping but she gave the princess a big smile. "No reason you can't learn."

Three speeches later, the princess was even more determined to learn how to do this, someday.

Bridget pulled on her sleeve. "Raise your hand for the Pepper Pot."

"What's a Pepper Pot?" The princess's hand was raised for her.

Mr. Giant in the front of the room banged his gavel. Bridget shrugged and mouthed the words. "You'll see."

"Wait!" The princess had a duty to her family. She flung herself into the breach. "I'll do it if you give me my workshop key and the keys to my tools."

"Some people don't know when to stop." Bridget untied her key ring and re-tied it on the side away from the princess. The princess put her arm down, but Bridget pushed it back up.

The first Pepper Pot was easy: "Name the kingdoms of the Mosel river valley, and tell us about your favorite."

As a Cochem princess, that would have been an easy question, but she didn't get that one. It went to a small-voiced person in the third row who only knew four of the ten, but made the best of it by describing his favorite—Cochem.

"This one's for the lady in the third seat." Mr. Giant pointed at the princess, and it felt like an electric shock. "Tell about a time when you did something you regret and what you did about it."

The first thing that came to the princess's mind was disguising herself as Nero at the christening. It wasn't something she wanted to talk about at all. She also hadn't done anything yet, to make up for it. "Um . . . ."

Bridget smiled at her encouragingly. The princess looked around the room and saw smiles everywhere.

They couldn't all be smiling *for* her. She looked down to see if she'd spilled something down her front or buttoned her sweater crooked, but her scullery maid uniform was spotless.

She gave a hesitant smile herself. "I played a prank on my family at my christening party." Everyone was still smiling, so she went on. "I pretended to be the guest we were waiting for so the parsnip fries wouldn't get cold."

There was a cheer from Peter the parsnip auctioneer. The princess smiled. It was easier to say something with people smiling and looking interested. They kept her afloat.

"But then some guests arrived late and were . . . *uh*, upset." The princess bit her lip and happened to look at the woman on the back bench who had said something about the youngest princess being a good-for-nothing prankster.

Bridget was giving the princess a funny look. But the whole room was waiting. "*Uh*, could you repeat the question?"

Mr. Giant repeated it.

In the back of the room, the timer held up a red card that meant she had to stop talking in 15 seconds.

The princess wasn't sure how much she could say in fifteen seconds, so she talked as fast as she could. "I helped put out the fire, and I washed a lot of dishes, but it wasn't enough."

She sat down, blushing painfully. The clapping kept her from sinking down in her chair, but she couldn't look up.

Giving this speech felt like the first time she'd pulled the lever for her dessert sluice in the hall. It might have been a disaster. But then water had filled the sluice and whooshed the little boats into every corner of the room. A speech was a lever.

But then a dummy on the back bench called out, "It could have been worse—what if your late guests were from the Blackfly Kingdom?"

Laughter reminded the princess that they didn't know who she was. Giving a speech with a fake name was like delivering cream puffs filled with shaving cream.

Bridget whispered in the princess's ear. "Don't pay any attention. Back benchers are too shy to give their own speeches, but they love to heckle people."

But Bridget didn't know who the princess was either.

Hot waves of embarrassment passed through the princess for the whole next section of the meeting so she didn't hear what they said about her speech.

Mr. Giant explained the evaluation part of the meeting. Four VVLers would tell tonight's speakers what they'd done well and how they could improve.

Talk about raising the bar. The princess's eyes widened. Now she was supposed to remember something she'd only half-heard AND say something about it? Forget the ice-covered mountain—a VVL meeting was like skydiving without a parachute.

"Don't worry so much!" Bridget patted her hand. "You have to sign up for those, they won't just call on you. Just listen and enjoy."

After a little while, the princess's heart stopped pounding, and she caught a few familiar things from past speech master's lessons. Mr. Giant was encouraged to speak softly sometimes, for contrast.

"Everyone can always hear you very well, so you don't have to worry about that." The laughter was friendly, and Mr. Giant laughed along with them, even pretending to laugh without any sound at all. It was easier to hear about other people's speeches.

Mr. Giant stood up to talk about the next speech. "Peter did a great job organizing his speech on one point—Parsnips!"

Everyone cheered.

"Peter told interesting stories and used his voice, his hands, and even his feet—" Mr. Giant mimicked Peter spading a garden "—to entertain us while we learned about parsnips. Maybe next time you could try a speech that wasn't about parsnips—"

"*Awwww*," protested the back benchers. "We need our parsnips."

When they'd finished, Mr. Giant went on, never losing his cool. "Excellent audience response, as always. Well done, Peter!"

The VVLers jumped up and clapped until the princess's ears rang. Her own hands burned from joining in. She'd never realized a speech was a tool, like a wrench or a hammer or a drill.

One speaker had all but tossed her notes in the air because she had rushed around so much during her talk. She was praised for keeping the audience involved. "Moving is good," said her evaluator.

Still trying to win Bridget over, the princess leaned over and whispered, "Why?"

"It kind of burns up the nervousness so you can talk."

Right. The princess looked at Bridget slant-wise.

Bridget's eyes widened. "It does—really! You should have heard her last speech. She could barely get the words out because she was shaking so much. Her chin was chattering. She did so much better this time. Try it yourself and see. Practicing at home—in front of the mirror—before you have to talk makes a speech go much better. If you have someone to practice in front of, that's even better."

That explained Bridget's outstretched arm in the dungeon before. The princess couldn't think of anyone she'd be comfortable practicing in front of, but it seemed like a good excuse for checking on the egg now and then. "How about a rook chick?"

Bridget's thoughtful pout gave the princess a sudden stomachache. "I'll lock you in with it as long as I can hear you practicing. As soon as you stop, out you go."

But the princess needed to come and go as she liked. Perpetual speeches in the dungeon wouldn't help her defend Cochem.

The Dungeon Master banged the podium with his gavel, and the room quieted. "A speech is a tool to entertain, to inform, to inspire, or to convince. Our evaluators are the tool-sharpeners. Let's hear it for our evaluators!"

The princess wrinkled her nose. A toolbox full of speeches was a funny thing to think about. How about a speech to convince Bridget to give up her keys? *Nah.*

A crack of thunder announced a storm breaking outside. Steady rain showered the Peppermint Tea House roof. The princess wished she'd shut the PAL windows.

Then a woman on the back bench said something a little nasty about the next speaker. The speeches and tips for speaking felt like a river, pulling the princess down. Bridget poked her.

Everyone in the room was looking at the princess. She straightened in her chair, bracing herself.

"Twyla, we're so glad you came to the VVL!" The Dungeon Master's familiar face looked down at her from the podium. "You've shown courage, standing up for the first time!"

Everyone clapped again.

Her smile grew. They were being extra nice because it was a club, but they had heard her.

The Dungeon Master made you feel like you could do anything. He would be the perfect person to head up a team to defend the castle. Look at the secret dungeon room he'd built overnight.

"I look forward to hearing your first speech." The Dungeon Master raised his voice to be heard over the rain on the roof. "The InterKingdom Speech Tournament is coming soon. ReVVLers, it's time to brush up!"

No, it's not. Forgetting everything but the Tournament, the princess fled.

"Hey!" Bridget called, and the princess remembered the keys.

She waited on the square to let Bridget catch up.

Rain bounced on the stone around the fountain and covered the square with deep puddles. The princess reached into her pocket and opened the scissors on her pocketknife.

"Thanks for waiting," Bridget said. "For a moment, I thought you forgot our deal."

"I did," the princess said. "But I remembered when I got outside." As soon as they were past the fountain lights, she planned to snip Bridget's keyring off its ties and run for it. Sneaking around the castle and hiding in corners was better than being locked in and useless.

One more step.

Scissors at the ready, the princess reached for Bridget's keyring, but then her clothes flickered, and she stuck her foot into the light, hoping for silver.

Blackfly princess slippers with a side of blackflies.

She looked up at once, ready to congratulate Nero on getting out of the dungeon workshop, but a much taller Blackfly royal glowered down at her.

Queen Ash.

Early for a change.

CHAPTER TWELVE
Early for a Change

STEPPING BACK OUT of the fountain lights, the princess tried to look past Queen Ash to see if the Cochem family had come home. Even in the rain, the princess could tell that no one in the queen's party wore silver. Her shoulders sank.

"Ho, there!" Queen Ash shouted right above the princess's ear. "What's the quickest way to Cochem Castle?"

The express stairway on the left got to Cochem Castle's front gate after a twenty-minute climb. The princess didn't hesitate. "Take the path on your far right, ma'am." That path meandered by a few scenic overlooks, crossed a giant field of stinging nettle, and ended in a bog.

If Nero was still in the dungeon, the princess needed time to throw him out.

"Stop! Shine the light there!" Queen Ash commanded and the Blackfly archers lifted their torches high so everyone could see the princess's Blackfly dress.

Bridget coughed.

"Who are you?" Queen Ash leaned down and stared into the princess's face.

Trying to give Nero every possible chance, the princess

said, "The christening you, *uh*, ruined with your archers. That was—" She pointed to herself.

"Nonsense," Queen Ash brushed away this explanation. "Blackfly princesses don't wait ten years to get a name."

Ouch. The princess swatted a blackfly on her arm and ignored Queen Ash's sting. Still stalling for time, she said, "I'm not a Blackfly princess."

"I don't like pretenders." The queen waved her hand and an archer held the princess fast.

"Now, you." The queen turned to Bridget. "Tell me where Prince Nero is."

The princess made all kinds of hand signals, but Bridget didn't or wouldn't catch on.

Bridget pointed to the express stairway. "He's visiting the dungeons, ma'am. Follow this stairway, and cross the garden to the dungeon. It's the quickest. Your archers might have to take off their helmets. The ceiling's a bit low in the dungeon."

The princess groaned. Nero was a well-educated prince. Why hadn't he figured it out? Hopefully, he was better at soothing angry queens than figuring out how to use a paperclip.

Held by the Blackfly archer, she couldn't even make a mad dash to the Fire Chief to try and defend the castle with the water pumps.

The whole party went up the express stairway and down to the dungeon, the archers helmetless. At the bottom winding, the ceiling was so low that Queen Ash's crown bumped it. The princess, sandwiched between the last two archers on the stairs above, had a perfect view.

"If you could take off your crown for just a moment—"

TROUBLE WITH PARSNIPS

Bridget said.

"Out of the question. I am The Crown. I never take it off."

If the queen kept this up long enough, Nero might still get out. A Blackfly reunion in the corridor would be the perfect chance for the princess to nab Bridget's keys and slip away.

"This is the only low spot, ma'am." Unfortunately, Bridget praised the ceilings of the *rest* of the dungeon.

"If you could take it off for one moment," Bridget coaxed, "I'm sure everyone would close their eyes until you had it back on."

The Dungeon Master's family was far too interested in hospitality.

After that, Queen Ash's party made quick progress. The princess's archer pulled her along and then stood in front of her, so she couldn't see. She shifted to the side.

The tiny window in the cell door clunked open, and Queen Ash called, "Nero? Are you in there?"

"Good morning, ma'am." Nero's head appeared behind the window grille.

The princess sagged against her archer's shoulder and was yanked upright.

Nero went on, "I didn't know you were coming to Cochem."

"There's a Tournament to be planned," Queen Ash said.

The princess wished she could wake up from this nightmare.

"If you go on up to the kitchen, Cook has some excellent roasted butternut squash tonight," Nero said. The princess gave him points for soothing remarks and noticed Bridget rushing away down the corridor. She might have early morning kitchen duty but the princess hoped she was going for reinforcements.

"Open this door!" Queen Ash rattled the cell door, but it didn't open. "Who dared lock up the Crown Prince of the Blackfly Kingdom?"

Nero gave Queen Ash an engaging smile. "It's training, ma'am, to break out of a dungeon using your wits. Very good for future kings, don't you think?"

Nero would be good at those Pepper Pots.

Queen Ash gave Nero a look as cold as the dungeon's stone blocks. "Where's the Dungeon Master? I want you out of here at once."

The queen ignored Nero's objections about fair competition or honorable behavior or royal skill-building. She shouted louder.

The Dungeon Master charged down the corridor to the cell and came nose to nose with Queen Ash.

The only acknowledgement he gave was an incline of the head. "I'm going to have to ask you to keep it down, ma'am. It's very early in the morning, and the dungeon guests need their peace and quiet. I won't have them disturbed."

The princess's mouth fell open. Maybe there was something to the VVL if it taught you to speak up to Queen Ash like that. The only other person who seemed able to talk to Queen Ash when she was angry was King Schwartz. Her anger didn't seem to upset King Oliver, but he never tried to tell her anything she didn't want to hear.

Judging from the deep purple shade of Queen Ash's face, the Dungeon Master's words were definitely in the category of things she didn't want to hear. She shouted, "Under WHOSE orders is my son in the dungeon?"

TROUBLE WITH PARSNIPS

"He was shooting arrows at the castle, ma'am." The Dungeon Master didn't even step back. The princess wanted to applaud.

"That's nothing," the queen said, preening herself. "I shot some arrows myself not so long ago. But no one's put ME in the dungeon."

The Dungeon Master looked regretful. "Unfortunately, I'm not sure we have a vacancy."

"Nonsense! Why would I want to stay in the dungeon?" The queen's archers sprang to attention.

"It's for training, ma'am." Nero's voice broke through the commotion. "My cousin's locked in too. It's a competition."

"Your cousin? Your cousins are all playing croquet."

The princess lost her faint hope that her family had merely been delayed. On the queen's other side, the Dungeon Master appeared to be taking a nap.

"Wait, what does this 'cousin' look like? Short and grungy with no manners?" Queen Ash hauled the princess forward in front of Nero's cell. "You mean this one? She told me the wrong way on purpose. She would have sent me right back through the nettle field that made us miss the parsnip fries at the christening."

Nero gave the princess a questioning look. She wiggled her fingers at him and gave him a sick smile.

His mouth took on a thoughtful shape, but he only gestured at the locked door. "I haven't figured it out yet, but I'm getting there."

Queen Ash spun the princess around, almost knocking over her nearest archers in the process. "YOU locked my son in the dungeon? How dare you!"

Queen Ash's eyes bored into her. Another second and the

princess would burst into flame.

"I wanted to try it," Nero said. "But look at her, if she's not my cousin, who is she?"

"I don't know." Queen Ash's foot tapped against the stone flags. She looked the princess over with distaste. "She says she's one of my nieces, but her name isn't Sibyl, and look how she's dressed. It's disrespectful."

"She's not a Cochem cousin. I think she's Melanie, from Minnesota. You know, in the New World." Nero's face disappeared. A tapping sound and his voice came out of the blackness. "She has her own blackflies."

"She has her own WHAT?"

"I didn't mean to offend you by mentioning–"

"Then don't," Queen Ash said. "Come out of there, come up to the hall, and talk to me properly. The only princesses they have in the New World are carved in butter at the State Fair. Besides, if she were Melanie, she would have said so."

The princess opened her mouth, but Nero was faster.

"She doesn't remember her name because she has a head injury." His voice was all edge. "If I had something that worked as well as a paperclip, I could help you, but I don't."

"Uh–" The princess had left him one.

Nero caught her eye and smiled. "That was part of the test, right? I threw it into the corridor."

He pointed through the grille at the stone floor outside the cell. Something glinted in the torchlight. Princes were a puzzle. The princess stretched down and picked it up. No wonder he hadn't gotten out yet. Her movement caught the attention of her archer who yanked her upright. The princess put the paperclip in her pocket.

TROUBLE WITH PARSNIPS

"Head injury? Paperclip? What nonsense! Dungeon Master, I command you to unlock this cell." Queen Ash pointed at it imperiously, in case he didn't know which one she meant.

The Dungeon Master yawned. "Oh, pardon me—I'm under King Oliver's and Queen Sibyl's orders, ma'am."

"As if Sibyl ever gave an order in her life." Queen Ash rummaged impatiently through her cloak and brought out the Golden Parsnip. "But I'm giving you one now."

The princess should have gotten Nero out of the dungeon right away. She'd given Queen Ash an excellent excuse to use the Golden Parsnip for whatever she wanted. The princess had let the kingdom down. The dungeon walls spun in an odd way.

Queen Ash grabbed the princess by her other arm and yanked. "None of that fainting stuff."

The princess took a deep breath and the corridor stopped spinning. Queen Ash had a death grip on one arm, and the Blackfly archer gripped the other. The princess's toes barely brushed the stone floor.

Nero's voice floated up from the floor somewhere. "Dungeon Master, I ask you most respectfully to leave the door just as it is. If you open it for me, it's cheating."

Queen Ash reached down through the bars of the grille. She laid her hand on Nero's forehead, and her voice rose to its normal volume. "If he has some kind of jail fever, heads will ROLL. Unlock this cell, Dungeon Master."

The Dungeon Master fit his key in the lock, but Nero held up a hand.

"No, no, I've almost got it. I just need one more minute." His head disappeared from the grille in the door.

The sound of tapping on metal meant he was jiggling the pins out of the hinges. That was the hard way, but it worked. A resourceful prince.

"You talked him into this nonsense. I command you to talk him out of it." Queen Ash glowered at the princess.

With the Dungeon Master right there, the princess had to speak up. "No, Ma'am."

Queen Ash shook the princess by the shoulders. The princess's chin banged against her chest. "You're not Melanie. For locking up the Blackfly crown prince, you'll be balancing on a board in the Blackfly dungeon until you fall off into the Rhine river."

From what Nero had said, a paperclip wouldn't do a thing. The Blackfly dungeon would be closer to her family, but she'd never get their attention if she were locked up. The dizziness came back, and the princess took a deep breath. She had to get away somehow.

"There!" The door was lifted off its hinges and walked backward, deeper into the cell. The grille framed Nero's face. He leaned the door against the wall and came around it, beaming at the princess. "You can learn anything with practice. It took me a while, but I finally got it."

He bowed over Queen Ash's hand. "Aren't you glad I can break out of a dungeon, ma'am?"

"I sent you here to secure the castle, not play games in the dungeon. Why don't you go tell your father all about it? I'm sure King Oliver would like to hear too." Queen Ash's long fingernails bit into the princess's arm, but it hurt worse to think about how angry King Oliver was going to be.

"In fact, take half of my archers, and set out at once."

Queen Ash was focused on Nero.

Nero's smile vanished, and the furrow showed up again. He bowed. "Is Princess Melanie coming with me, ma'am?"

Brilliant idea. The princess gave him full points.

"No, I'll keep *Melanie* here with me." Queen Ash's fingernails bit deeper, and the princess gritted her teeth. "We have a lot to catch up on."

"Oh." Nero gave the princess a half-smile and an encouraging, chin-up sort of look that sent her courage into her socks.

"Nero? I'm waiting." Queen Ash folded her arms.

Nero's face turned pink, and he headed out. The princess watched him go, feeling like she'd been abandoned by a favorite brother.

When the sound of their footsteps had faded, Queen Ash called out to the Dungeon Master. "Send me word at the hall as soon as that door's fixed. *Melanie* is planning an extended stay."

The princess fingered the paperclip in her pocket. Three minutes, tops.

After commanding two Blackfly archers to stand guard over the princess, the queen and her remaining retinue swept past. The princess small preparations to safeguard the castle were useless. The Fire Chief wouldn't give the bearer of the Golden Parsnip any problems, and blackberries couldn't hold back a troupe of Blackflys.

The Dungeon Master set to work with his tools. "Don't worry, ma'am, we'll do everything we can to make you comfortable."

As long as Queen Ash had Cochem Kingdom in her pocket, the princess didn't see how, but she gave the

Dungeon Master a wan smile. Friends in low places were valuable.

"Oh, Dungeon Master, one more thing," the queen called. "Before you lock her in, search her for paperclips." She waved the Golden Parsnip. "That's a command."

The princess rubbed her aching forehead.

CHAPTER THIRTEEN
Dungeon Hospitality

The Dungeon Master sent one of the Blackfly archers to get Bridget, while he re-hung the cell door. The princess offered to hand him tools, but he politely turned her down. So much for getting him to let her into the secret room.

The remaining Blackfly archer guarded her while the Dungeon Master worked, so no one said much at first. If Queen Ash had taken all of her archers, the princess wouldn't have to stand here looking like a Blackfly page. She unbuttoned the jacket and turned the lapel back to cover the Blackfly insignia. So far, the Dungeon Master didn't seem to care what kind of prisoner she was, but it felt awkward.

"*Uh*, it's about the PAL."

"Hugh's been called away." The Dungeon Master grunted and threaded the heavy door neatly back onto its hinge pins.

"When . . . is he coming back?"

The Dungeon Master's mouth twisted, and the princess was sure he knew something. "I think it'll be awhile."

"Excuse me, sir." Shutting the door in the Blackfly

Dungeon Hospitality

archer's face, the Dungeon Master slid the bolt back and forth to make sure it still matched the doorframe.

A neat way to get rid of the Blackfly archer.

"*Uh*, I was wondering . . ." The princess re-tied her apron more snugly and wished she could turn off this disguise.

Focused on the door's moving parts, the Dungeon Master moved his oil can to every squeaky spot. "What is it?"

Before he opened the door again, she had to ask. Even if it was the wrong thing to say. "Since no one is taking care of the PAL, can we, *uh*, hide the rare books?" The princess pointed towards the fake wall but didn't say "secret room" out loud.

The Dungeon Master turned to her for the first time since he'd closed the door. He blinked. "Bridget told me you did that."

The princess opened her mouth to ask her question again but the cell door opened, and Bridget came in with the Blackfly archer.

"So now we're searching pockets?" Bridget exchanged a look with her father.

"Change of management." He meant Queen Ash.

As soon as Bridget came over to the princess, the page outfit sprouted a scullery maid apron.

"You're making me flicker," the princess whispered. She ran to the bed and slid underneath.

"Hey–" Bridget's feet and then her face appeared.

Bridget called back over her shoulder. "Gentlemen, I'm going to need privacy for this new policy."

The Dungeon Master ushered the Blackfly archer out and went out after him. The princess came out from under the bed.

Bridget went systematically through the princess's pockets, picked out the sole paperclip and the pocketknife with scissors—"I'll keep these"—and handed the princess a ball of string, a small screwdriver with a cork, and a tiny notebook with pencil. "You keep weird things. Kind of like Fifteenth, but since you're not Fifteenth, you'll be staying in here."

"But—" the princess didn't want any Blackfly archer to know there was a secret room or a rook egg under a brooder either. She murmured, "You could give me the key so I can . . . *uh*, practice."

"Prisoners don't get keys." Bridget glanced at the open door to the corridor and lowered her voice. "But I can come back and let you practice for a little while later."

The princess risked another question, "Do you know where Hugh went?"

Bridget gave her a sharp look, and the princess wondered again what the secret was.

"Even if I knew you were Fifteenth, I wouldn't lock you in there." Bridget slanted her eyes towards the fake wall. "I'm not going to let Ms. I-Am-The-Crown come down here and find no one. Or find something in here that she shouldn't see . . ."

"She won't come down," the princess whispered. "She doesn't like taking off her crown."

Bridget glanced over at the men first before speaking. "But she always wants the Dungeon Master to do things for her. She'll come looking for him."

"Not in the morning." The princess tilted her head towards the fake wall. "You can lock up after breakfast."

"The dungeon doesn't serve breakfast," Bridget made a

grimace and imitated Queen Ash's manner. "'Royals sleep at that hour, and prisoners can do without.'"

The princess would be willing to ignore her growling stomach if she had the rook egg. "Lock up before lunch then."

Bridget hesitated, and the princess tried to sweeten the bargain. There had to be a Harold or a Sibyl who could join the VVL. "Maybe you could get your ribbon."

"Deal." The huge smile on Bridget's face made the princess feel guilty and nervous at the same time. "But only in the morning."

"Uh, it's morning now," the princess said.

"Have some patience," Bridget said. "Gentlemen, I'm ready."

The Dungeon Master, the archer and Bridget went out of the princess's cell and locked the door behind them.

※※※※

A quarter of an hour later, the key turned in the lock again, and Bridget appeared and unlocked the secret room. "Hurry up—I have dishes to wash."

"If you gave me the keys, it would save you a lot of trouble."

Bridget's eyebrows went up, and she put the key back into the keyhole. "Should I forget the whole thing?"

The princess took one look at Bridget's face and dragged out the brooder. Bridget locked the secret room again and gave the princess a piece of cinnamon crumble cake wrapped in a silver napkin.

"When I come back, you'd better have a speech for me." Bridget went out. "I'm not doing all this for a back bencher."

The princess cuddled the egg on her lap and took a

blissful bite of cake. She wondered if the rook chick could already hear. She held the egg to her ear.

Nothing.

She stroked the pebbly surface of the egg with a careful finger. "Will you be friends with me? Even though I don't have a name yet, I am a real Cochem princess. I'll call you Calypso."

She cupped the egg in both hands and earnestly tried to convince the rook chick inside that she was the Fifteenth child of Cochem.

⁂

For the princess, the only good thing about the next two days was the constant stream of castle staff bearing boxes of books from the PAL. "Have you seen her?" an under-gardener asked on the first day.

"Seen who?" The princess took a box from the pile near the cell door and carried it to the back wall.

"You know—the Blackfly princess. Have you seen her around?" The under-gardener picked up a box and followed her.

"Uh, yes." As much as her ever-changing disguise allowed, the princess kept her story the same.

The next afternoon, Cook stopped short in front of the princess's reading table. "Prisoners don't get library privileges, do they?"

"Uh, no." Unfortunately, the princess wasn't lying. She still didn't have a library card. "Those are Prince Nero's books."

Cook didn't budge, so the princess added, "Hugh Ancry gave the Blackfly prince a PAL library card, *uh* . . ." What reason would make sense to Cook? ". . . oh, *uh*, as a gesture of InterKingdom friendship."

Dungeon Hospitality

Cook snorted, but she set down Cochem's rare recipe collection and went out of the cell. After that, the princess made sure Nero's books were covered up before anyone came in.

Twice a day, Bridget showed up with circles under her eyes, practically sleepwalking. The princess always ran to take her tray before she dropped it.

The Dungeon Master wasn't around at all. Queen Ash must be running the dungeon staff ragged. Lately, Bridget was working too hard even to ask the princess about speeches.

They set up a second brooder so it was quicker to move the egg back and forth. When it wasn't in use, the princess threw a blanket over it.

Once the secret room was unlocked, the girls pushed the deliveries in, so everything from *Bee World* to *Nematode Behavior* was safely stowed.

The rest of the time, the princess got into the habit of talking to the egg so the chick would know her voice. She didn't have any tools, so she couldn't make anything. She had to talk things out instead, like how to prove her identity, get her carrier pigeon messages, and keep from vanishing. A rook chick was a perfect audience. No snickering, heckling, blank looks or snoring.

Sometime during her second night in the dungeon, the princess realized two things. First, Bridget wasn't going to just bring messages for Fifteenth down to a page-scullery-maid-Blackfly-princess in the dungeon. Messages might be lying somewhere in the castle unless Queen Ash had burned them.

Second, the princess only had five more days before she

vanished. She threw off the covers and walked up and down in her cell.

⁂

At midnight, the princess was startled by the key turning in the lock. Blowing out the brooder lamp, she snatched up her covers and threw them over it. Queen Ash shouldn't see the egg.

But Bridget brought in a tray with rolls, butter, blackberry jam and two steaming cups of hot chocolate with whipped cream crowns.

"Wow." The princess's stomach made embarrassingly enthusiastic noises.

"Queen Ash didn't say anything about midnight snacks. And if I try to eat in the kitchen, there's always something else to do." Bridget stood waiting, and the princess cleared the books away from the table to make room for the tray. They each took a cup and clonked them together.

"To Cochem!" The princess wished she could put the dungeon staff in charge of Tournament refreshments. "Do you serve invisible people this much too?"

"Invisible people? We've never had any or are you trying to say we'd never notice if we did?" Bridget gave the princess a funny look. "Are you feeling okay?"

"Never mind." Only Hugh knew about the invisible part which meant the princess would starve if she vanished while living in the dungeon. She put extra jam on a roll and took a bite. "Have any messages come for Fifteenth?"

Bridget paused with the cocoa pitcher in mid-air. "Why do you want to know?"

"*Uh*. I'm not actually a scullery maid under the spell of a Blackfly prince." She had to prove it. "I'm the youngest

Dungeon Hospitality

Cochem princess. King Oliver is my father."

"Princess Soapsuds strikes again," Bridget set down the pitcher. "Spies don't get refills."

The cocoa was going to Bridget's head. The princess tried again. "I sent invitations to the Bishop and to the Seven Kingdoms for the christening. Did any answers come?"

Bridget looked at her sideways and shook her head. "Have you got a fever? I can call the Cochem physician."

"I'm fine." The Palace Physician couldn't cure *hiding in plain sight*. "What if I tell you what's in the messages? Will you believe me then?" So far, the rook egg had been a much better listener.

"Nero told me a rock hit you in the head, and you told me he was casting a spell on you." Bridget shrugged. "But if you were a Cochem princess, you'd look like one, at least some of the time. Sorry, I don't think I'm going to help you read other people's messages. Nothing personal."

The princess couldn't blame her. Bridget's caution reminded the princess of the way the Cochem siblings were kept out of her dungeon workshop. "I can prove it. Ask me about anything in the workshop, and I'll tell you what it's for."

"How will that prove anything? You saw it all when we got the brooder out," Bridget said.

Still missing her hex wrenches, the princess gave her a sour look. "Only the stuff you filed under L, O, W, and C."

"Okaaaaay." Bridget described things in the workshop, and the princess explained the jig for making baskets, the hooks for the cable ferry, and the silk panels of the hot air balloon. She'd been sewing silk and building a frame for months, and the hot air balloon was almost finished.

"Then there were some things with long tubes. What are they for?" Bridget asked.

"Oh. The ones in the corner with the tiny silver balls? I don't know." Covered with dust, they'd been sitting in the workshop for as long as the princess could remember.

Bridget grunted. "If you were a Cochem royal, you'd know what a Speaker Meter looked like."

"I'm not a speaker," the princess said, but Bridget didn't look convinced. The princess took out her cable ferry sketch. "This is what all those pulleys are for."

"That looks brilliant," Bridget said. "I could visit my grandma every afternoon if we had a ferry like that across the Mosel. If you're really the youngest princess, why don't we have one yet?"

Because Harold had a math test, but the princess couldn't rat on her brother. She frowned. "Not enough cable."

"Okay, maybe I believe you. Flip the switch or whatever you do, and make yourself look like a Cochem princess." Bridget looked expectantly at her.

"None of my siblings are around, so I can't look like myself."

"If you say so." Bridget folded her arms. "Does Nero do this too? Or is he actually a Blackfly prince?" There was a fluttery sort of something about the way she said prince. "Maybe I should get him to cast a spell on me too."

The princess widened her eyes so she wouldn't roll them. Royal fever was silly, but it was rude to say so. "No, he's a Blackfly all the time."

"Too bad," Bridget said and yawned so hard her jaw cracked.

The princess waited. It felt like Bridget almost believed

her.

Bridget put her hands on her hips and fixed the princess with a hard look. "If you're really Fifteenth, tell King Oliver or Queen Sibyl Cochem needs another scullery maid. Queen Ash is using every plate we have."

The princess winced. Getting her parents' attention was the problem. There had to be a way she could help Bridget. She smiled. "In my workshop, I can build you a machine with whirling brushes and flying soapsuds that can wash pots faster than Cook can make them dirty."

"If you can make one, I'll take it off your hands." Bridget refilled the princess's cocoa, but she went away without letting the princess near her tools.

CHAPTER FOURTEEN
The Second-Best Croquet Mallets

THE PRINCESS DIDN'T see Bridget again until lunchtime the next day.

"Sorry about the no breakfast thing." Bridget made a face in the direction of the Blackfly archer, still standing in the open doorway. He shut the door, and she set down her tray.

In a beautiful silver bowl, croutons floated on a sea of steaming, creamy soup.

"That smells so good!" The princess continued her Convince-Bridget-Campaign. "but what I really need is my–Fifteenth's–mail."

Bridget pulled a tube out of her pocket but held it out of the princess's reach. "This came today from King Oliver, but I don't know who it was for. The name at the top is all smeary. It must have been raining."

"What does it say?" The princess forced herself not to reach for it. Grabby didn't help.

"We're back to reading other people's messages," Bridget said. "What kind of a dungeon do you think this is? We follow the IKCDC."

The Second-Best Croquet Mallets

"If no one reads it, how will you know who it's for? It might be important."

Bridget frowned, unrolled the message and read. She shook her head. "I can't tell who it's for."

The princess took a deep breath. This kind of talking was very hard work. "Can I guess what it says?"

Bridget's face was a mask. "Okay, guess."

"King Oliver's on his way home?"

Bridget's hand went up in a noncommittal way. "Anybody could guess that."

The princess slumped down in her red velvet dungeon chair. "He's too busy playing croquet to come home."

Bridget's expression changed. "That's actually pretty close."

The princess pulled up her knees and wrapped her arms around them, hiding her eyes as if she were inside an egg. Her parents weren't coming.

"Guess again." Bridget nudged her. "You might get it. Don't give up."

The princess picked up her head. Did Bridget believe her? Or King Oliver needed something, and she wanted him to have it. "He forgot the black painted croquet balls?"

Bridget looked from the princess to the message.

"Well?" The princess frowned.

"He needs the second-best . . . something, something." Bridget stared at the princess, as if this was a Pepper Pot, a spy code for black-market parsnip sales, or a password for rook egg smuggling.

The princess jumped up. "The second-best croquet mallets!"

"Yes!" Bridget reached over, shook the princess's hand as

if they were at the VVL meeting, and showed her the message.

To the most esteemed ~~SMEAR SMEAR.~~
 Urgent: Please send the second-best set of croquet mallets.
Oliver
 King of Cochem, etcetera, etcetera.

The princess turned over the message to see if he'd written anything on the back. Nothing. The princess had been feeling sorry for her family because they all had the fever, but this felt worse.

King Oliver had played so much croquet he'd worn out the croquet mallets—and during all that time—he still hadn't noticed his youngest daughter wasn't there?

The princess held out her hand. "Give my your keys—I need my drill and the exploding glitter. When he gets these mallets, he's not going to forget me in a hurry."

"Make me an alphabetical list," Bridget said.

Cochem must have the most cautious dungeon staff in the Seven Kingdoms. Normally, that wasn't a bad thing. The princess made a list, and Bridget brought her everything on it.

"I wouldn't mind seeing that in action." Bridget stood by the door, holding the tray with dirty dishes.

The princess drilled a hole in the face of the white mallet, filled it with exploding glitter, and fitted a neat plug into the hole to hold it all in. "I wouldn't either."

When Bridget came back, a few hours later, the princess finished the final seam in the hot air balloon silk, knotted it, and bit off the thread. She packed the mallets into the hot air balloon basket and dusted glitter off her hands. "That should do it."

Bridget ran her hand over the colorful silk of the balloon and beamed at the princess. "I'm sure no one but Fifteenth could have made this. If you keep this up, you're going to convince me."

The princess pointed out the correct line on the wind chart to Bridget. "If you ask the Fire Chief, he ought to be able to light the burner and launch the balloon. If he launches it at 18:00 and lets it go up 800 meters before he releases it, the wind should blow it straight over to the Blackfly Kingdom. Can you send a carrier pigeon over to let them know it's coming?"

"Will do. I can't wait to see it go up." Bridget clapped her hands.

Once King Oliver knew the mallets were coming, he would chase them all the way to France or if the balloon fell short, he would set out towards Cochem to get them. If the princess could tie a string to them, she could fish for her family.

Bridget pulled a handful of message tubes out of her apron pocket. "These came for you too."

"*Uh.* Thanks." Bridget almost believed her, but the princess's mood sank. How long had the messages been waiting? The first one was from the Bishop, who accepted Cochem's kind invitation.

"The Bishop is coming." One down. Only the Seven Kingdoms to go. The princess made a chalk-mark on the wall of her dungeon. "That helps."

"Bishop?" Bridget coughed.

"For the christening," the princess said, more patiently

than she could have before the rook egg.

"But that's what got the castle burned down in the first place."

The princess put Bridget fully into the picture, beginning with how she'd disguised herself as Nero and wrapping up with Kizzy's christening gift.

"You mean without a name, you just blink out like a light?" Bridget asked.

The princess nodded. There wasn't anything more to say.

Bridget humphed. "What's in the other ones?"

The next six were from the secretaries of the other six kingdoms. The Magenta Kingdom was still recovering from smoke-induced illness. The Saffron Kingdom had urgent business they couldn't put off. The Indigo Kingdom didn't even give an excuse.

The princess read them all a second time to make sure.

"That's so rude." Bridget sat on the end of the bed.

"None of them are coming." The princess had a feeling of unreality.

Bridget prodded her with the feather duster. "The way I see it, the Tournament is the answer to all of your problems, so what's your problem?"

"Uh." The princess didn't have one problem with the Tournament. What she had was wobbly knees, a tendency to blank out, and a naturally quiet voice. With Cochem full of speech makers, she wouldn't have the smallest chance to make herself heard. "I'd have to practically give a speech to get King Oliver and Queen Sibyl to remember to give me a name."

"A christening speech! Brilliant!" Bridget said, as if she'd been waiting for the princess to make that suggestion.

The Second-Best Croquet Mallets

"Now I know why Hugh asked me to help you prepare for the Tournament. Just imagine how annoyed your aunt will be if you beat Nero and bring the Velvet Purse home to Cochem."

"Yeah," the princess said, even though beating Mr.-Crown-Prince-I've-had-lessons-for-years Nero was impossible. "She'd probably burn down the castle all over again." A christening would never fit between the end of the Tournament and the beginning of Queen Ash's tantrum. An invisible princess would have an even harder time rescuing the castle the second time.

Bridget moved the books onto the bed and picked up a dusting cloth and a spray bottle of Gleaming Dungeon furniture polish. "It's a heck of a lot more fun to have a pet rook, if the rook can see you. And you could finally get your own library card. Seems worth it to me."

The princess huffed. Hugh, Nero, and Bridget all talked to her as if she could re-invent herself. She didn't have any more control over being heard than she did over her magical disguise. "Of course it would be worth it," she said, "if I were the kind of person who could do speeches."

Bridget stared at her. "Weren't you paying any attention at the VVL meeting?"

The princess didn't see what the VVL had to do with her. "They're all good at it."

Bridget snorted. "That does it. I'm taking you to Speech or Die tonight."

The princess wished Queen Sibyl were here to hold her for a moment. She picked up the warm egg, held it in cupped hands, and forced herself to think about a beautiful cable ferry across the Mosel.

Or one hung from a cable in the air. But even the magical image of people traveling smoothly in the air from one kingdom to another didn't slow her galloping heart.

"Wait till you see Mr. Giant. He does a speech that's a complete stitch." Bridget started laughing, fell over onto the bed, and kept right on until she slid slowly onto the floor. The princess helped her up.

"We always have Speech or Die before the Tournament. It reminds people how much they've already learned." Bridget beamed, as if the princess had thanked her for a wonderful birthday present.

The princess had that sick feeling you have when someone expects you to enjoy a present you know you're going to hate. She gestured at the cell walls and hoped she looked properly regretful. "Queen Ash won't—"

Paying no attention, Bridget got the Blackfly archer in the corridor to carry the improved croquet mallets and the hot air balloon parts and left, calling over her shoulder, "Gotta get this in the air by 18:00."

The archer was already gone when Bridget dashed back and stuck her head in the door. "I'm only doing this because you're coming to Speech or Die tonight. Promise me, as a princess of Cochem, that you're coming."

The "princess of Cochem" part made the princess say, "I promise. Golden Parsnip Word of Honor."

The princess spent the rest of the afternoon and early evening reading books about rooks and cable ferries without taking anything in, and worrying about Speech or Die.

Bridget had laughed so much. It couldn't really have anything to do with dying, could it?

On the other hand, standing up in front of a room felt enough like dying that it didn't make much difference. The whole thing made the princess shudder.

Bridget had made her give her word as a princess of Cochem. She probably thought the princess would make a dash for freedom. Well, Bridget was right.

CHAPTER FIFTEEN

Speech or Die

THE WAY FROM the dungeon to the Peppermint Tea House felt much too short. In the VVL meeting room, Bridget made the princess sit in the front row. So much for slipping out the back door.

"Are you sure I don't have to sit on the back bench?" The princess wished she hadn't done that Pepper Pot just because they were all smiling at her. They'd probably smile her to death tonight.

"Positive." Bridget grabbed hold of the back of the princess's neck and pushed her head down. "Now breathe. Your face is the wrong color for any kingdom. Tonight will solve everything. Once you do Speech or Die, you'll be so ready for the Tournament—you can't even imagine."

Bridget was right. The princess couldn't.

A huge banner decorated with skeletons and knights of the realm spelled out "Speech or Die!!" in letters taller than the princess. She took a deep breath.

"Are there Pepper Pots tonight?" The princess tried to sound more interested in answering them than avoiding them.

Speech or Die

"Later. By Royal Command, we have them at every meeting."

"Why's that?" Anything to keep Bridget talking.

"The Pepper Pots are a way to keep everyone in shape. You know, for the InterKingdom Tournament."

The princess didn't know. That's why she was here and not in the dungeon. She wished the rook egg was in her pocket instead of securely locked up in the secret room.

"Well, there's a Pepper Pot Duel option, if something shady's going on." Bridget smiled. "It's part of why there is a VVL at all. We're a defense against silenced voices."

The princess tried to imagine silent people defending themselves against a noisy Queen Ash and failed. "Like what kind of cheating?"

Bridget waved a hand to include the whole room. "Oh, any kind of cheating. The challenger calls out that they want a Pepper Pot Duel against the host or hostess. The winning speech is the one that causes the strongest audience reaction. Whoever wins can call for any change in the Tournament except a complete Do-Over."

"How about cancelling the whole thing?"

"Oh, I don't think so." Bridget gave her a hard look. "But after tonight, you won't be talking about cancelling. Speech or Die is too much fun. Anyone giving a speech in the Tournament is allowed three minutes. You're going to love it. Oh, since you didn't say 'Fifteenth' last time, I thought you might not want it, so I put this instead." Bridget pointed to the middle of the program.

Twyla of Cochem.

That wasn't really her name, but the princess wasn't taking any chances. She leapt out of her chair and took off down the aisle to the exit. She hadn't signed up for the Tournament, and she wasn't going to risk dying. She'd only agreed to come because Bridget had finally recognized her. The princess had given her word as a princess of Cochem that she'd come.

Well, now she was retreating.

"Mr. Giant," Bridget called. "We've got a runner."

The princess came face to knee-caps with the huge Mr. Giant blocking the door. He knelt on one knee and held her arm gently between thumb and forefinger. "You don't want to miss Speech or Die." He seemed to be under the impression that he was whispering, but his voice carried through the whole room and probably all the way down to the Mosel. Heat rose in the princess's face. "It can change your life. Try it. You might like it."

He turned her gently around and nudged her towards the front row. Since his idea of a nudge had quite a bit of force behind it, the princess found herself at the stage before she could get her feet under her. She sat down at the opposite end of the front row, but Bridget slid down and whispered, "Don't be angry, but I think I'd better sit next to you before you get some disguise that's hard to explain."

Bridget was right so the princess didn't move, but she didn't answer either.

The Dungeon Master went to the front and smacked his gavel on the podium. "Welcome, VVLers! Let Speech or Die begin!"

Bridget had told her once that moving helps burn up nervous energy. Since the princess clearly couldn't flee, the only possible move was clapping. She clapped with everything she had, ignoring her stinging palms.

Speech or Die

Much to her surprise, the next thing that happened was the Dungeon Master crouching down behind the podium. Bridget and the others wore expectant smiles. A bloodthirsty crowd. The princess swallowed hard.

"Ladies and Gentlemen, fellow VVLers, welcome guests . . . " The Dungeon Master's voice came from behind the podium, but she still couldn't see him. The princess craned her neck. As she watched, he seemed to grow slowly taller than the podium, but since he was reading from a scroll held in front of his face, he was completely hidden.

"Hospitality in a dungeon is very important. But some people think it isn't important at all. Maybe they are right too."

The Dungeon Master was always so clear when he spoke, but this speech was like a spiderweb. He seemed to be arguing with himself.

"The most important part of dungeon hospitality is safety. But if a dungeon guest doesn't have a good experience, it doesn't matter how safe it is. So the most important part of dungeon hospitality is a comfortable bed and good food. Unless . . . " He went on to contradict himself a few more times.

Fingers appeared at the top of the scroll and rolled it up without ever showing the Dungeon Master's face. He and the scroll vanished behind the podium. There was a moment's silence and a storm of applause.

The Dungeon Master popped up and bowed. "Watch out for rabbit holes." The whole room of VVLers stood up and clapped. The princess only joined in because Bridget pulled her up.

Mr. Giant was the next speaker. The first thing he did was

pass a basket to the front row. When it reached the princess, she saw it was full of foam cores.

"Earplugs," Bridget said with a smile.

That seemed rude to the princess, but everyone else was stuffing them in their ears. Her earplugs were still in her hand when Mr. Giant opened his mouth. The first sentence of his speech rolled out like an earthquake.

Stunned, the princess sat there pressed against the back of her seat. Bridget put the earplugs in the princess's ears. Blessed relief. Mr. Giant's voice filtered through at the perfect volume. After giving Bridget a thumbs up, the princess gripped her chair to keep Mr. Giant's first point from sweeping her away.

Three minutes later, everyone in the room was clapping standing up, stomping their feet in enthusiasm. The princess couldn't stand it. Mr. Giant was going to get his feelings smashed to smithereens. With that speech, even the princess knew he would lose the Tournament. Afterwards, he'd have to buy hearing aids for the entire Seven Kingdoms.

He was beaming in the front, catching the stage curtains with every perilous bow. He put his finger to his lips and mouthed the words: "Watch your volume."

Oh. She'd been so worried about people's feelings that she'd missed the point of the meeting. Tonight's speeches were about how NOT to give a speech. She whistled and clapped with everyone else. This kind of speech might be possible, even for her.

When the room subsided, the princess took out her earplugs, copying Bridget. "What's next?" she asked, almost comfortable for the first time since they'd sat down.

"You are." Bridget held up the program and pointed to her name, but this time she held on to the princess's arm.

"No, I'm not." As fast as the princess peeled Bridget's fingers off her arm, Bridget clamped them down again.

She spoke right in the princess's ear. "Last time, you answered a Pepper Pot, but a speech doesn't work from the middle of the room. If you want people to know you are a princess of Cochem, this is the first step. You have to walk to the front." Bridget let go of her arm.

The Dungeon Master was looking right at her with a question in his eyes. The princess could shake her head, and he would go on to the next person. Or she could do this.

She swallowed and met the Dungeon Master's gaze with a tiny nod. Her heart pounded but she struggled to her feet and somehow got to the end of the bench.

The dungeon master banged his gavel on the podium. "Please help me to welcome our next speaker, Twyla of Cochem."

The whole club clapped. The clapping was like a wind blowing on her back, pushing her forward to the podium, where the Dungeon Master clasped her hand.

He supported her elbow with his other hand. "There's nothing like Speech or Die for the first time." His voice was soft and kindly, and somehow she managed a quiver of a smile.

"Take a breath first," he said. "Makes it much easier."

Then he sat down, and the princess faced the room. She took a breath.

Bridget fixed her with a determined gaze from the second row as if she was holding her up by force of will.

TROUBLE WITH PARSNIPS

The others looked at the princess expectantly as if they wanted to know what she would say.

"Good evening, VVLers." The princess's mouth quivered, and she took another breath. "Thank you for having me." She had no idea what to say next. Then she remembered what the evaluator had said at the last meeting. "I look forward to hearing your speeches." She looked at the Dungeon Master for help. He came over and shook her hand.

The whole room burst into applause, and the princess took her seat, dazed. Everyone was smiling at her. Well, the back bench was probably making fun of her, but all of a sudden it didn't matter.

She might never get a name, and she might vanish, but she had seen the view from the front of the room.

Her arms and legs were shaking, but she could sit in her seat until it stopped.

The experience was so heady that when Bridget handed her the official entry form for the InterKingdom Speech Tournament, the princess took it.

The first line was NAME. This wasn't a nametag. An Entry Form was an official document. She couldn't just write Fifteenth Child of Cochem. That wasn't a name. That was why she needed stage time in the first place.

Her handwriting was full of odd loops and wiggles because her hands were still shaking, but she didn't care. *Hiding in plain sight* wasn't going to win. She was going to give a speech, and get a name of her own. Buzzing with excitement, she wrote the name hoped for: *Twyla, in spe*; Twyla, in hope. When Hugh found out about this Entry Form, she hoped using her Latin would shock him into coming home.

With shaking hands, she folded her entry form into a paper airplane and sent it sailing forward. It nosedived into the entry basket.

Bridget stuck her whole arm in the basket and stirred it in. The princess gulped. What had she done?

※※※

To: Hugh Ancry, Royal Librarian of the Palace Agricultural Library

Dear Sir,

My Entry Form for the InterKingdom Speech Tournament is in the Basket. I hope your urgent library business is going well.

Sincerely,

15th

Princess of Cochem

P.S. FOUR MORE DAYS TO SEE ME AT ALL.

P.S.S. EVER.

P.S.S.S. UNLESS YOU BRING MY PARENTS

※※※

On the way back from the VVL, it was so early even the stars looked tired. The princess and Bridget stopped by the dovecote and sent a message to Hugh.

When they got to the princess's cell, Queen Ash was in the dungeon corridor. She seemed to be trying to bend a paperclip with the dungeon door, but she straightened up fast and put whatever it was in her pocket. That looked like a security leak to the princess.

Queen Ash looked the "Blackfly" princess up and down. "Out for a little walk?"

"Exercising the prisoner, ma'am." Bridget must have

answered a lot of Pepper Pots in her time. The princess wanted to clap and run away all at the same time. After all these days, she'd been sure Blackfly royal visits were a thing of the past.

But Queen Ash had gone to the crown-adjusting trouble of visiting the dungeon in person at the crack of dawn, when her archers could have brought the princess to her.

"Is there something I can do for you, ma'am?" Bridget asked the question the princess was wondering. She unlocked the cell door, and the princess went in.

"I came down to find your father, and no one was home." Queen Ash looked down her nose at Bridget. "Give me your key—I'll lock up."

When Bridget didn't, the queen held the Golden Parsnip in front of her face. "Forgetting something?"

Bridget gave the queen a single key and the princess an apologetic look and went.

The princess eyed her royal aunt. She hoped Queen Ash still thought she was Nero's cousin, Melanie, from America. Threatening an American Blackfly with the Golden Parsnip was pointless.

Queen Ash whipped the blanket off the brooder lamp. "There's a heat wave in Cochem. What are you doing with a heater?"

The princess hoped the queen wouldn't give her a direct command to tell the truth. "For a hot air balloon?"

"Wrong answer." Queen Ash had her hands on her hips, and her foot was tapping.

The princess's heart beat faster. "Nero said there was storm damage, ma'am," she said, copying his confidence. "The cell had to dry out."

Speech or Die

Queen Ash's foot stilled, and the princess wondered if she'd gotten away with it.

"Nero wrote asking if the egg had hatched yet." Queen Ash held up a message addressed to Melanie of Cochem.

Oh. The princess winced. Without a name, mail was a real problem.

"So where is it?" Queen Ash bent over the brooder. "Rook eggs are for Cochem royals, not for Blackflies."

If the queen saw the egg right now, she would find out about the secret room, the rare PAL books, and that the dungeon staff holding out on her. That would probably cause an dungeon-shattering explosion.

The princess wasn't about to let that happen. "But you're a Blackfly, ma'am."

"At least I used to be a Cochem royal, which is more than you can say." Queen Ash looked down her long nose at the princess. "Your country doesn't believe in royalty."

Queen Ash could command the princess to give her rare books or the key to the secret room. But a rook egg didn't hatch on command.

"The egg will only hatch for a Cochem princess," the princess said, doggedly. "Right now, I'm the only one in the kingdom." The sentences she'd said over and over again to the rook egg unspooled like cable. "The Fifteenth Child of Cochem" came out of her mouth automatically, as if someone else had said it for her.

"Say that all you want, but I'll never believe you." Queen Ash picked up the brooder lamp and shook it as if the egg might be hidden inside. "You look nothing like any Cochem princess I've ever seen. I have the Golden Parsnip, so why shouldn't it hatch for me?"

The princess's mouth fell open. She didn't know if the Golden Parsnip was enough to hatch a rook.

Putting down the lamp, Queen Ash looked under the armchair. "If you think about it, Cochem Castle is the perfect home for the Blackfly family. Black rooks sailing over a nice, sooty black Tower. It's all wasted on a family with silver banners. Besides, I was the only Cochem princess in my generation. I'm one-of-a-kind."

Queen Ash preened, and a cloud of blackflies swirled around her. "A rook chick has to like ME best."

"What if the Golden Parsnip isn't enough? Why risk it?" The princess had to stop Queen Ash somehow. "I could—"

"I'm not risking anything on a fake Cochem princess." Queen Ash pointed an accusing finger. "You're not hatching a rook egg and taking it off to America where it will probably catch a nasty disease."

The princess had seven sisters who were Cochem princesses. She must know some way to prove she was one too.

No one in the kingdom knew her. Without any of her family, she didn't look or sound like herself. This fairy godmother gift was going to cost her family the kingdom. She groaned.

"I didn't think so." Queen Ash put Bridget's key into the keyhole and unlocked the door. "I shouldn't have sent that scullery maid away. She won't give me trouble when I command her to give me the egg. She's from Cochem."

Uh, oh. The princess had to think of someone even Queen Ash would have to believe. Right away!

CHAPTER SIXTEEN

The Queen's Wager

"ANOTHER THING." QUEEN Ash's back was to the princess. "I'm not going to ask what you were doing out of this cell, but I noticed. The Dungeon Master had better have a good explanation."

The Dungeon Master had to follow Golden Parsnip commands just like Bridget. To protect the rook egg, the princess had to prove her identity right away. "Wait—who's your fairy godmother?"

"Fairy godmother?" The queen's head turned. "What does a butter princess like you know about fairy godmothers? And if you say you're the Fifteenth Child of Cochem again, I'll spit."

The queen's angry face was nose-to-nose with the princess, who took a quick step backward.

Skipping over the Fifteenth Child of Cochem part, the princess went on from there. "My fairy godmother has micro-braids and likes red sneakers. Her name is Kizzy."

"Did you say . . . Kizzy? But your hair is blacker than Nero's." Queen Ash yanked the princess's hair. "No, you must be a spy."

TROUBLE WITH PARSNIPS

As soon as the queen let go, the princess stepped back. "No, ma'am. It's a gift from Kizzy."

"Keziah Akosombo!" Queen Ash flung her arms out wide, and her voice reverberated in the small dungeon cell.

A moment later, Kizzy appeared on the table full of books, rubbing her ears. "You don't have to shout."

The princess's mouth dropped open. So that was how you got your fairy godmother to show up.

Kizzy sat down on a PAL reference volume and crossed her ankles, swinging her red sneakers gently to and fro. She looked up at Queen Ash. "Things not going well in the Blackfly Kingdom again? I warned you about the blackflies, but you wouldn't listen."

The princess was interested, but Queen Ash's hand swept that topic away. "See anybody else here you know?"

Kizzy swiveled around, shading her eyes and peering out under her hand as if she were on a stage in the floodlights. "Oh, it's the youngest Cochem princess! Nice outfit." Kizzy giggled.

Ignoring Kizzy, the princess squared her shoulders and faced Queen Ash. This was her chance to protect the rook chick. "This, *uh*, proves I'm a Cochem princess because we have the same fairy godmother."

Shaking from effort, the princess gulped for air and braced herself for some terrible order enforced with the Golden Parsnip.

"Sixteen of them get croquet fever, and there's STILL one left over to plague me." Queen Ash covered her face with her hands, then glowered at Kizzy. "Trust Cochem to have an incompetent fairy godmother. What you're saying is, it's all up to the parents. It's not like I can get a new name now to get rid of this charming gift you gave me." She flicked her sleeve, and a cloud of blackflies poured out.

"We've talked about making a name for yourself before." Kizzy waved her magic wand, and the blackflies flew in single file out the cell door window.

Stunned that the queen hadn't instantly reached for the Golden Parsnip, the princess couldn't take in what Queen Ash was saying. "You always were better at making messes than fixing them."

"Do you really want to talk about your mess?" Kizzy smiled sweetly at Queen Ash, who looked away.

Kizzy turned to the princess. "I'm really sorry. I can't seem to remember your name."

"That's because I don't have one."

"You don't?" Kizzy's tiny forehead creased with worry lines. She took out her fairy book and started frantically looking things up in the index. "Name . . . no name . . . page 6555."

The princess held her breath. She didn't want to talk about her visibility problem where Queen Ash could overhear.

Kizzy flipped to the page and ran her tiny finger down the lines, her wings opening and closing nervously the whole time. Finally, she slammed the book shut. "Get one quick."

The princess was grateful Kizzy hadn't said anything about invisibility out loud. "That's what Hugh said."

"Hugh, your librarian?" Kizzy asked. "Wonder how he knew that?" She referred to a tiny pop-up calendar. "That takes you to the 15th."

Three more days. The princess rubbed her arms and

TROUBLE WITH PARSNIPS

wondered if invisible hands worked as well. Not being able to build things would make a lonely invisible life harder.

"I want to know if she's going to STAY like THAT all through the Tournament." Queen Ash pointed at the princess, sketching an X in the air with her finger as if she could make the princess vanish by crossing her out.

The princess shuddered. She had to make sure Queen Ash never found out how easily vanishing could be arranged.

"I. Can't. Tell. You," Kizzy said, in an extra patient voice. "It depends on which name she gets."

"Don't be difficult." Queen Ash's eyes narrowed. "Everyone KNOWS what name she'll get."

"Could you look up Calypso and Twyla?" The princess had to risk it in case she never got another chance. Both names had the royal Y and the royal L of all Cochem princesses, and neither name was Sibyl, but the princess had no idea what magical qualities they had.

Kizzy sat down on the edge of the podium, opened Volume 2, and looked in the microscopic index. The princess flipped her telescope around, but it couldn't handle such tiny print. She watched Kizzy's face instead.

Whipping out a pair of black opera glasses, Queen Ash looked over Kizzy's head as the fairy flipped pages. "Don't go by the A's so fast!"

Queen Ash clearly thought this was about her.

"Calypso, here it is. Page 13,456." Kizzy found the page and ran her finger down it. "Calypso means hidden. Not recommended with ... Oh, really? I hadn't remembered that part." She turned back to the index. "'Twyla, woven with two threads ... not bad, not bad at all. Let me just

The Queen's Wager

check. *Hmm-hmm hmm hmm hmm.*"

Kizzy didn't say "hiding in plain sight" but her *hmm*'s had the exact same rhythm. Fairy godmothers must have some idea of confidentiality after all.

"What does it say?" This time, the princess was getting all the details.

"If you take the name Twyla, the wild type will latch onto one thread, and the domestic type will latch onto the other." Kizzy gave the princess a triumphant look.

"That means I'll *uh,–*" the princess didn't want to say invisible in front of the queen–"'blend in' sometimes?"

Kizzy nodded. "Twyla blocks the expression of the wild type. You'd be able to choose when you want to blend in and when you want to stand out."

"What does 'blend in' mean?" Queen Ash asked, and the princess held her breath, but Kizzy didn't explain.

Huh. The princess wriggled her shoulders, as if she was putting on a new sweater. Except for the part about learning to speak up for herself, Twyla felt like a good fit. She wasn't jumping to any conclusions. "What about Calypso?"

Kizzy shook her head. "That's not so good. Calypso means hidden so you'd have the wild-type."

Meaning, even with a name, the princess would be invisible. After her experience with *hiding in plain sight*, she didn't want to be hidden.

The rook chick could keep the name Calypso. Vanishing into the sky was probably an advantage for a bird of prey.

The queen's eyes narrowed. "Wait a minute, how do we know you're telling the truth? You told ME gifts can't be changed."

TROUBLE WITH PARSNIPS

Everyone else was much better informed about fairy godmother gifts than the princess. When she saw Hugh next, she was going to ask him to order some books for the PAL. But then she remembered that most children were christened before they could read. Books for parents, then. She couldn't understand why he hadn't sent a message.

Kizzy shook her head. "The gift must have taken some kind of nickname for a real name—"

Fifteenth wasn't the sort of nickname the princess wanted to keep all her life.

Kizzy went right on, "But unless she's christened by the Bishop with a real name in front of the Seven Kingdoms and her royal parents, there's not a thing I can do about it." Kizzy stood up, spun on her heel, and vanished.

Huh. Fairy godmothers were really a lot more trouble than they were worth. Too bad you couldn't ban them from royal christenings.

"If you're a true Cochem princess . . ." Queen Ash cocked her head to one side. "Why can't you put two words together without sweating blood? All the Cochem children are excellent speakers."

The princess would have liked to know the answer to that one too. She mopped her forehead with her handkerchief.

Queen Ash pulled out Bridget's dungeon key.

Uh, oh. The princess couldn't let Queen Ash lock her in and take the key away.

"Can I, *uh*, help with the . . . Tournament?" The princess shuddered. She was bound to defend her kingdom to the death—or to the InterKingdom Speech Tournament—which was basically the same thing.

Queen Ash looked back over her shoulder. "A Cochem

princess who looks like a Blackfly isn't exactly help. You'd wander the castle and give orders that would ruin everything."

That was sort of the princess's plan, but it made her sound like the kind of double-agent who got locked into the dungeon for life. "*Uh*, I don't always look like a Blackfly princess."

"I've never been so fascinated in my life." Queen Ash yawned. She turned the key in the heavy lock and pulled on the door. "You'll stay in the dungeon until the Tournament is over. It's safer."

The princess disagreed. Life as a starving, invisible prisoner wasn't safe at all. She had no plans to become a ghost. "Wait—I can . . . I can look like a princess from any of the Seven Kingdoms."

After a long, considering look, Queen Ash set her pocket sand glass on the table. "That could be useful. You have one minute to show me." She flipped over the glass, and the black sand flowed down. "Starting now!"

"I have to be near the royals of whatever kingdom," the princess stuttered over her words. "Then I look like them." She pointed from Queen Ash's black gown to her own.

Queen Ash grabbed hold of the princess's wrist and pulled her out of the cell. "This, I have to see." As she rushed the princess up the corridor, she said, "If you're lying, I'll lock you up for the rest of your life and that won't be very long."

The princess had already figured that out.

꒰ࠥ꒱ࠥ꒰ࠥ

When Queen Ash and the princess came out of the dungeon and into the daylight, tents were going up in the

TROUBLE WITH PARSNIPS

Cochem Royal Campgrounds.

It smarted a little that the guests had come for the Tournament after turning the princess down, but then no one had ever won the Velvet Purse at a christening. At least this way, Queen Ash thought everything was about the Tournament. The new christening invitations had probably flown right over her head.

Seven Kingdoms. *Check.*

The Cochem family's arrival shouldn't cause any suspicion. Bridget might help keep Nero and his father supplied with cream puffs after they arrived. With their mouths full of whipping cream, they wouldn't be able to mention the invitation.

The Bishop, on the other hand, was a dead giveaway. The princess just had to get to him first. She checked the sky for returning carrier pigeons, letting Queen Ash pull her across the grass.

Nothing.

"Would you stop studying the clouds?"

"Yes, ma'am." The sky was empty of news. The princess might as well watch her step on the slippery shale in the vineyards.

Queen Ash dragged her down to the campground and shook her arm. "You still look like a Blackfly to me. Get on with it."

This had to be about the Golden Parsnip. Why else would the queen care?

"*Uh.* I need to have a little ... space." The princess pointed at the colorful tents. "I can't look like them if I'm standing next to ..." She waved a hand at the space between the queen and herself.

The Queen's Wager

Narrowing her eyes, the queen dropped the princess's wrist. "I'll be right behind you."

As Regent of Cochem, Queen Ash probably wanted to make sure the only resident Cochem princess wouldn't put her out of a job.

No danger of that.

No matter what the princess did to make the guests feel welcome, no one would see her as a Cochem princess.

Uh, oh. The Indigo tent was up, but deserted.

The Saffron Kingdom's campsite was still in-progress. The princess's dress turned yellow as she came up to their tent.

"Good morning, ma'am." With her now blonde hair falling in her face, the princess dropped a curtsy to Queen Saffron. "Anything I can do to help?"

Queen Saffron smiled at the princess, vaguely, as if she were trying to place her, and then her mouth turned down as her gaze continued over the princess's shoulder. "If it isn't Queen Ash. To what do we owe this honor?"

From where she stood, a meter or so behind, Queen Ash lifted up the Golden Parsnip, and her mouth stretched into a grimace. "I'm the hostess of this Tournament."

At that moment, a Saffron princess came out of the tent, knitting in hand. Seeing Queen Ash, she ducked right back in.

Next to the princess's ear, a voice whispered on the other side of the yellow canvas.

"Queen *Ash?*" said a loud voice that sounded like King Saffron.

"Shhhh!" said several voices at once.

CRAACK! The tent suddenly developed a lopsided shape.

"What'd you do that for?" it sounded like Princess Saffy's brother.

"If we don't have the right pole, we'll have to go home," King Saffron said. "What a pity."

Uh, oh. They couldn't do that.

Next to the princess, Queen Ash's face looked like a thunderstorm ready to boom.

"Ma'am, I'd be honored to make you a new tent pole," the princess curtsied to Queen Saffron again. "It shouldn't take long, once I have the measurements."

Swatting blackflies, Queen Saffron lifted the tent flap and cleared her throat. "Saffy? We have an offer for a new tent pole."

The Saffron princess came out of the tent again, waved a few more blackflies away with her knitting, and looked the princess over from head to foot. "Why would you do that? Who are you?"

"I'm . . . oh, never mind." Nothing the princess could say would be believed. "I'd hate for you to leave."

"You can't LEAVE. You'll spoil everything." Queen Ash took a step forward, looked at the princess's flickering dress, and stepped back again.

Odd.

Queen Ash must want to keep the princess's disguise secret. But it didn't make sense. The princess wasn't a good speaker like her siblings, so the magical disguise couldn't help the queen cheat, and this wasn't Speech or Die, where you could give a bad speech on purpose.

"Please, ma'am," the princess said to Queen Saffron. King Oliver expected his children to be hospitable. "Don't go home without a new pole."

The Queen's Wager

Leaning over, Queen Saffron whispered in the princess's ear, "You look like one of us, but I don't know you. Do you speak for . . . ?" Queen Saffron's eyes indicated Queen Ash, who was absorbed in ticking off some kind of diabolical list.

The princess whispered, "for King Oliver." Then she took her tape measure out of her pocket, pulled out the tape, and let it snap back in, like a lizard's tongue. "Can I?"

Princess Saffy lifted the tent flap. "Be my guest."

A few moments later, the yellow imposter princess came out again, jotting numbers down in her little notebook.

"That was quick." Princess Saffy looked up from her knitting.

"I'll bring them by later." People were easier to talk to when the princess had something to offer. She hoped she could get the keys she needed to keep her promise. "Has anyone seen the Indigo family?"

"They're up at the hall with the Rose Kingdom," Princess Saffy said.

The princess thanked her and started figuring out how she could get up to the hall. If the Bishop was in the hall too, she really wanted to get there before Queen Ash.

The queen was watching from a spot half-way to the Magenta tent. She jabbed a finger at the back of the Saffron tent, tracing the route she meant the princess to take. The one that ended right in front of her.

In hopes of keeping Queen Ash at a distance, the princess saluted to show she'd understood.

The Magenta Kingdom's tent looked oddly bunched up. Their motherly queen was sitting in a hot pink Adirondack chair next to the tent's doorway. The princess hurried towards her.

TROUBLE WITH PARSNIPS

Gathering up the skirts of her suddenly pink dress, the princess dropped a curtsy. "Good morning, ma'am."

A puzzled frown appeared on the Magenta Queen's face. "Do I know you? I thought I knew all the Magentas."

The princess hoped she hadn't seen the change from yellow to pink. She changed the topic right away. "Do you need something for the tent?"

The Magenta Queen's face cleared. "I'm not supposed to tell, but you're one of us, so . . . King Pink seems to have forgotten the tent pegs. All 57 of them. Right after he caught a glimpse of you-know-who." The Magenta Queen tipped her head in the direction of Queen Ash.

"Maggie! I told you not—" King Pink came around the side of the lumpy Magenta tent and stopped short when he saw the princess. "Wait, you're not a Blackfly."

"No, sir." The princess plucked up her pink skirt and curtsied. The thought of tent pegs steadied her. "I've got some 12-inchers, if that helps."

"Thanks, but we're actually on our way out." King Pink coughed and looked pointedly at Queen Ash, who stood a double arms-length away, swinging the Golden Parsnip back and forth. "This tent isn't fire-proof."

The princess needed the Seven Kingdoms to stay but she had to keep them safe. She pointed to the silver tent with a red cross between the Mosel River and the campground. "You could put your tent next to the firefighters."

"That's not a bad idea," Queen Maggie said. "The kids really do want to give their speeches. Check your toolbox again, Pink. Maybe you missed them."

King Pink turned as rosy as his name. "I'll check one more time. At least Cochem has a good firefighter brigade."

The Queen's Wager

The princess took a hasty departure from the Magenta tent, promising to be back with whatever tent pegs she had. She didn't have to know if King Pink had really forgotten his tent pegs. A princess could recognize a diplomatic answer when she heard one.

In the middle distance, Queen Ash pulled out her sand glass and tapped it, meaningfully. Then she moved over towards the Marigold tent, leaving just enough space for the princess to go by without turning into a Blackfly. A shade too helpful. The princess wished she knew what Queen Ash was up to.

When the princess got to the Marigold Kingdom, they had their reasons for leaving at the ready.

"If we had even a comic strip left, we'd stay," Queen Studentenblume said.

King Rugosa agreed. "No one's seen the Cochem family, and even their Royal Librarian isn't here. That's no kind of hospitality. What are we all supposed to do while we're waiting? You can't even check a few facts."

"Be right back," the princess said and took off for the castle.

The PAL's Reference Section was in no shape for visitors. What an inconvenient time for Hugh to have urgent library business! She'd forgotten that the speakers liked to do last-minute fact checking. The PAL was the best library in the Seven Kingdoms.

The rare books and magazines were hidden in the dungeon's secret room, but the Harolds' royal washroom alone had a huge collection of comic books, fiction and non-fiction. She passed an empty wheelbarrow and went back to get it, pushing it up to the castle keep as fast as she could.

"Come back here!" Queen Ash was panting from the climb, but she raised one arm, and Blackfly archers surrounded the princess.

The princess stopped where she was, holding the stitch in her side. "Didn't you hear, ma'am? I have to get something for them to read or every one of the Kingdoms will be gone by tonight."

"No one gives up their chance at the Velvet Purse because they don't have enough to read." Queen Ash had never been a book person.

"Uh, some people get nervous while they wait . . . um, to give a speech," the princess said. "Or they need to check a fact for a speech."

"Is that so." Queen Ash's eyebrows went up, but she commanded her archers to fill the wheelbarrow with every magazine and newspaper they could find in the castle, and deliver it to the campground. The first archer pried the princess's fingers off the wheelbarrow, and the others filed into the castle behind him.

The princess followed, but Queen Ash pulled her back. "Not so fast. You and I are going to have a little talk. You're going to enter the InterKingdom Speech Tournament."

The princess's stomach lurched even though she'd already entered.

"You're going to give six losing speeches."

Instinctively, the princess fled, but one of Queen Ash's archers tackled her almost immediately. Lying on the grass, the princess imagined herself—speechless—on six different-colored platforms, surrounded by the royals of each Kingdom. A rainbow horror movie. In comparison, Speech

The Queen's Wager

or Die was a stroll down the Mosel.

"This year there are only seven speeches, one from each kingdom. It will save lots of time." Queen Ash dusted her hands together as if she hadn't just insulted the princess and proposed cheating the entire Seven Kingdoms. "Nero will give the seventh, winning speech."

"*Uh, no.*" The princess hoped her magical disguise had thrown up enough dust that Queen Ash wouldn't immediately pull out the Golden Parsnip.

"You mean 'yes.'" Queen Ash put on her black glasses and inspected the princess over the top of the frames. "Or I'm going to tell all Seven Kingdoms that the InterKingdom Tournament is off. No Velvet Purse. They'll all go home. Are you sure that's what you want?"

Ouch. The colorful tents would be rolled up in minutes. The royal families of the Seven Kingdoms wouldn't be back for years.

The princess would be invisible by then. Shading her eyes with her hand, she looked up at Queen Ash. Had someone told her about the christening?

But then she realized what the queen's plan would mean. Cochem Kingdom would never live down the disgrace of tampering with the Entry Basket. The princess hunted for the flaw in the queen's plan. "If the guests figure out there's no chance to win the Velvet Purse, they'll go home anyway."

"Then you'd better make sure they don't find out." Queen Ash breathed on her long, black fingernails and buffed them on one sleeve. "For every speech you don't give, I'll tell King Schwartz to put one of your family members in the Blackfly dungeon." Queen Ash smiled in a how-do-you-like-that sort of way.

TROUBLE WITH PARSNIPS

"Why?" The princess didn't know what else to ask.

"Why?" Queen Ash swirled her arms in the air, and a cloud of blackflies came out of her sleeves. "Of all people, you should understand. The Velvet Purse is going to get rid of this dratted fairy godmother gift. I've got my eye on an exterminator from Poland. Quite handsome, but very expensive."

Busily swatting, the princess said nothing. Even if Queen Ash won the Velvet Purse, she was going to be disappointed. A regular exterminator could never wipe out magical blackflies, and the Velvet Purse wouldn't interest a fairy. Magical people wanted Nectar, not gold coins.

A disappointed, blackfly-yielding Regent was a serious danger to Cochem Kingdom. The princess had to buy some time for her family to get over their croquet fever.

A sticky wicket.

"Okay," the princess said as if the queen couldn't make her. "On one condition."

"Condition?" Queen Ash laughed. "I have the Golden Parsnip, and a Cochem princess wants to make a condition?"

"The key to the, *uh*, dungeon." The princess had to look after the Seven Kingdoms guests, keep tabs on the queen, and intercept the Bishop.

"If you need a little security blanket, why not?" Queen Ash tossed the key—out over the moat. "I can get what I want from a Cochem princess, anytime."

The princess took a flying leap, caught it, and fell in with a splash. When she surfaced, Queen Ash was gone. The princess swam under the drawbridge and clambered out of the moat, shivering even though the day was hot.

CHAPTER SEVENTEEN
The Entry Basket

Trailing moat water and duckweed, the princess stood for a moment in the entrance to the hall, trying to get her bearings. So far, she hadn't spotted the Bishop.

Splat! Splat! Splat! The plasterers were covering Cochem's hall with some kind of dark plaster. That was a bit more than the usual Tournament commotion.

POP! POP! The Blackfly archers were getting in some target practice with black balloons. The princess covered her ears. If her parents got here, they'd never be able to hear. As much as she hated to admit it, a speech was the right tool for the job.

Squeak, squeak. Queen Ash pushed open the hall's famous squeaky doors. She was calling for parsnip fries.

A blob flew through the air and struck her black skirt with a *splat*, blending right in.

"Watch what you're doing, you nincompoops!" she shouted. Queen Ash was turning the hall into a giant chalkboard.

On the far end of the dais, a party of Rose and Indigo royals sat around the table, chatting and eating parsnip

TROUBLE WITH PARSNIPS

fries. The princess was glad to see them making themselves at home.

Not wanting Queen Ash's attention, the princess used the plasterer's scaffolding to get to a spot near the dais where the Entry Basket stood.

A clump of people from the VVL's back bench were putting the Entry Forms into neat stacks and checking them off on the official speaker's list. The back benchers were doing their part.

Then Queen Ash strode up to the Entry Basket. "Just the people I wanted to see."

The ventriloquist's dummy in Darnell Brummer's hands sniffed and turned his head away. "What's THAT Queen doing here? We want King Oliver and Queen Sibyl."

For once, the princess agreed with Darnell's dummy. King Oliver and Queen Sibyl should be here to receive the Entry Forms. Queen Ash wasn't the Tournament's hostess, only the organizer.

Queen Ash held up the Golden Parsnip. "I've got everything under control. There's one teensy, weensy detail. Prince Nero—my son and the Blackfly Crown Prince—is brilliant, but he's not good with maps."

The princess winced. She would hate if her parents said things like that in public. Fortunately, the VVLers weren't listening. They were arguing about whether they should take the Entry Basket away again.

Queen Ash cleared her throat. "We have to move the Tournament back a day to give him more time to arrive."

What? The princess jumped up onto the dais.

"You could have dried off first," Queen Ash said. "I wasn't in a hurry to see you again."

The Entry Basket

The princess stood on tip-toe and whispered, "Ma'am, you can't move the Tournament back."

"Can't I?" Snapping her fingers, Queen Ash spoke at full volume. "It's already done."

The princess had a choice. Keep quiet and vanish. Or speak up and tell Queen Ash she was spoiling her own plan.

Still whispering, the princess said, "If you move the Tournament, my, *uh*, disguise won't *work* anymore. It's in Kizzy's book."

"Well, take a vitamin or something." Queen Ash waved one hand in the air. "I can't change it. Nero can't win the Tournament if he isn't in it."

Taking a deep breath, the princess admitted the worst. "But ma'am, it'll make me invisible."

"Are you telling me Kizzy gave you an *invisibility* cloak?" Queen Ash's eyes narrowed to slits.

That wasn't quite right, but the princess went with it, hoping the VVLers were too busy debating to overhear. "Imagine what it will look like, ma'am. No one will believe there are invisible princesses in all Seven Kingdoms."

Queen Ash scowled. "We'll tell them it's an epidemic."

"But ma'am, they'll pack up and go home before the first speech."

"Stop being difficult." Queen Ash's eyes narrowed. "You're trying to get out of our bargain, aren't you?"

"No, ma'am."

"I didn't think so." Queen Ash measured her with a look.

The princess thought of something that might help her christening along too. "If Nero came with King Oliver and Queen Sibyl, he couldn't get lost."

"Oh, no, not Oliver." Queen Ash patted the Golden

Parsnip. "But one of those Harolds or Sibyls they've got so many of . . ." She scribbled a message and gave orders for it to be sent to the Blackfly Kingdom.

Feeling like she'd successfully dodged disaster, the princess went to the Indigo and Rose end of the dais to see how they were doing.

From there, she'd also have a good view of the entrance, in case the Bishop arrived. She could run over and bustle him off before Queen Ash noticed.

Once the Bishop was in Cochem, the princess had to make sure he didn't leave. He probably wouldn't approve of a christening tacked-on to a crooked Tournament. The princess wasn't crazy about it either, but it was the only way.

Beaming at the Indigo and Rose royals, she sat down between an Indigo prince and a Rose princess. Her dress flickered between Blue and Blush.

"Welcome to Cochem!" she said.

"Are you sure about that?" The sweep of the Indigo prince's arm took in the riot of plasterers, the VVL group with the Entry Basket, and the Blackfly archers practicing their aim on black balloons.

POP! POP!

The Rose princess jumped. "The Tournament is happening in Cochem this year, right? We are in the right kingdom, aren't we?"

"Yes, yes—it's just . . . repairs." The princess picked up a silver teapot from the dais. "Peppermint Tea?"

Splat! Splat! Splat! The plasterers were still working.

"That's another thing." The Indigo prince took the cup with a gracious nod, but his eyebrows came together.

The Entry Basket

"Where's the Cochem family? I need to do a little fact-checking in the PAL and it's not open."

"*Uh.*" The princess blushed, noticed her dress flickering again and stepped closer to the Roses. Blush wasn't any closer to Silver than Blue and she couldn't offer the PAL. Instead of facts, she offered the prince a platter of Cochem's favorite food.

The Rose princess leaned forward and whispered, "I heard the *Blackflys* got library cards."

Uh, no. Cook must have told the Fire Chief about Nero's library card. By the time the fire fighters told the gardeners who told the stable staff who told the guests, the whole Blackfly family had cards.

"I don't believe it." The Indigo prince crunched a parsnip fry. "Hugh would never do that."

Relieved, the princess re-filled his plate with parsnip fries.

"He's not even here," the Rose princess said. "And you know that Blackfly princess in the dungeon? The one nobody ever heard of before? Well, she has REFERENCE books. It's not fair."

The princess pulled herself together. It was too late to stuff parsnip fries in the Rose princess's mouth.

In spite of the racket, the Indigo prince looked around as if he wanted to make sure no one else was listening. "If Hugh is gone, then maybe it's true. I heard the books are—" he mouthed "disappearing" and cut his eyes towards Queen Ash on the other end of the dais.

"Noooo," the Rose princess said in a voice oozing horrified enjoyment. "She wouldn't."

Before the princess came up with any words to defend

Cochem's honor, the whole group of Indigo and Rose royals got up and drifted out of the hall.

Resting her aching forehead on the table, the princess tried to think of a way to quash these rumors before all Seven Kingdoms packed up and went home in a huff.

At that moment, Queen Ash pulled an Entry Form out of the basket and read it aloud. "Fifteenth Child of Cochem, Princess Twyla? There's no such person."

The princess picked up her head so fast, she knocked over the teapot. A pool of Peppermint Tea appeared on the tablecloth. She grabbed for a napkin.

"Hey, Queenie, you can't take things out of the Entry Basket. You're not from Cochem and you're definitely not a VVLer!" Hildy's ventriloquist's dummy didn't even bother to throw in a ma'am.

Queen Ash paid no attention. "There's no such princess. Every last one of them is called Sibyl."

The princess's lips pressed together in a grim line. Queen Ash knew perfectly well there was a Fifteenth. They'd just had that whole thing with Kizzy in the dungeon.

"This Entry Form is FORGED." Queen Ash was digging through the Entry Basket and tossing Entry Forms everywhere. She dusted her hands together. "Clearly, I have to do the Entry Forms myself."

Grinding her teeth, the princess longed to snatch up the Entry Basket and hide the Entry Forms in the secret room, but Queen Ash would wave the Golden Parsnip and demand them back. For now, the princess's resistance had to stay underground.

The VVLer with the Entry Basket protested. He was the only one without a ventriloquist's dummy. "But ma'am, our

The Entry Basket

charter says that only the VVL can sort the Entry Forms."

"Yeah—King Oliver signed it himself." Darnell Brummer's dummy pulled a scroll out of Darnell's pocket and unrolled it in the queen's face.

Not bad for a back bencher. The princess unclenched her jaw. Not bad at all. If they could learn to speak up like that ...

Queen Ash seized the scroll, slashed it again and again with her tiny dagger, and threw the ribbons in the fire. "Charter? What charter?"

The princess was dumbstruck. Slicing up a two-hundred-year-old charter was a terrible thing to do.

Hildy's dummy found her voice first. "That's not fair! You can't do that!"

"Of course I can. Until Oliver is back, I'm in charge here." Queen Ash pulled out the Golden Parsnip and waved it in front of Hildy's face. "And if any of you want a chance to compete in the Tournament, you'll mind your step. Oh, and one more thing."

The queen took the Entry Basket from the stunned VVLers hand and dumped all the Entry Forms onto the hearth fire, smothering it.

Watching the queen's plan play out was worse than the princess had imagined. How could she make this right again for all those speakers? She needed her family in the worst way.

Tendrils of smoke curled around the edges of the Entry Forms.

"Distribute these around Cochem for me." Queen Ash handed out stacks of flyers to the Entry Basket team. "It's just the sort of thing you VVLers are good at. Who knows?

If you do it well, I might be interested giving you a new charter."

The VVLers went out of the hall, grumbling, and the hearth fire recovered enough to send up a thick plume of smoke. A horribly familiar stink made the princess's eyes water.

Plasterers fled in all directions, opening all the big doors as they went. Blackfly archers ran out after them.

One of Queen Ash's flyers fluttered onto the princess's slipper on her way out. She picked it up.

Save 50% on your next AirCastle stay!

The flyer gave her an idea. Once she was outside, she flipped it over and read the printer's information on the back. Royal Printer of Cochem. No reason to let Queen Ash have everything her way.

Maybe Queen Ash's fake Entry Forms could be printed on rice paper. Then if the princess accidentally-on-purpose dumped water on them, they'd dissolve, or the ink would wash off.

Oh, what a shame.

⁂

As soon as it was dark, the princess climbed to the top of the Tower and launched the emergency flares. The rockets whooshed across the night sky, and burst, spelling out: "GET WELL FASTER" in red, blue, and green sparks.

The grand finale shimmered silver:

COME HOME.

No one had shot off emergency rockets for the past fifty years. She hoped they'd get her family's attention now. Then she went down and locked herself safely in the dungeon for the night.

The Entry Basket

❧❧❧

To: Royal Printer of Cochem
Dear Madam,
I'd like to place a rush order for 15 InterKingdom Tournament Entry Forms printed on rice paper and another 700 on regular, Entry Form paper. Please deliver to the Cochem dungeon.
Many thanks!
15th
Princess of Cochem
P.S. Please send the bill to King Oliver.

❧❧❧

To: Nero, Crown Prince of the Blackfly Kingdom
Dear Cousin,
Queen Ash won't start the Tournament until you get here.
7 Kingdoms will pack up if T. doesn't start.
Need 7 Kingdoms and my parents for christening.
Is Hugh reading a book? He's not answering my message.
Please help.
15th
Princess of Cochem, Melanie, Sibyl #8

CHAPTER EIGHTEEN
A Library Crisis

ALL NIGHT LONG, the princess dreamed about standing—speechless—behind colorful podiums above a snickering crowd. She woke in a cold sweat on the morning of the 13th.

Shudder.

As soon as the Seven Kingdoms figured out all six princesses were fakes, the next disaster would happen. They would chase her right out of the Seven Kingdoms for helping Queen Ash steal the Velvet Purse. She couldn't blame them.

On the other hand, if she didn't make it perfectly clear who she really was—the nameless princess of Cochem—she couldn't be baptized, and no one would ever see her again. Her disguise made it impossible to look like herself until her family showed up.

There was no way around it. She needed six solid speeches.

"Well, really, I need seven," she told the rook egg by the warm red glow of the brooder lamp. "Six fake ones for Queen Ash and one real one for my parents and the Bishop."

To give herself time to think, she made a detailed

drawing for a Tournament platform with a trap door, for speakers who needed to escape in a hurry. It didn't help.

"How will I ever come up with seven speeches?" She started with the Saffron Kingdom. "Hi, *uh*, you always see us knitting in the Saffron Kingdom because we're industrious. We're the busiest in the Seven Kingdoms."

The princess sighed. Maybe Indigo was easier. "Hi," the princess shook her head. Much too quiet.

"HI."

That was probably right, because it felt like shouting.

"I'M THE . . . INDIGO PRINCESS." Her voice got softer and softer, because she kept forgetting to make it loud. "THE LONG-LOST one, just visiting from SOMEWHERE where there are EXTRA Indigo princesses kicking around." She whispered, "Like extra princesses do—" caught herself, and stopped. No one was going to need foam earplugs for her speeches.

She put her face in her hands. After a moment, she forced herself to get up, and went over to the rook egg.

"You've got to help me." The princess cupped the egg in both hands and looked down at its beautiful surface. "Hi. My speech is about the beautiful parts of the Seven Kingdoms." Then she kept on talking, without having any plan, just caught up in the egg and pretending someone else was giving a speech. She was just listening.

Speaking like this wasn't so different from hiking through the vineyards. You stayed on the main path to keep out of the stinging nettle.

Say one thought until it was finished. "What's beautiful about Cochem? The way the rooks wing over the Cochem Tower on a sunny day in spring. Cherry trees blooming pink along the sparkling Mosel River. Squeaky kitchen doors that make everyone's stomach growl. Everyone crunching parsnip fries at all the tables in the hall."

If she could say something like that for the Tournament, she wouldn't embarrass her family, if they were there.

As an imposter, giving speeches about the nicest things in each kingdom wasn't a bad idea. If King Oliver couldn't stop the crooked Tournament in time, maybe the guests wouldn't be as angry.

"Hi," she said to the rook egg, this time pretending to be a Marigold princess. "We're a little bit shy in the Marigold Kingdom." The Marigolds had dived under their table for shelter at the first hint of the Duel of the Halls. "We're the kind of people you can invite to a party without worrying if we will behave ourselves."

"Hi." Bright pink was so loud, it sort of held you up. "The Magenta Kingdom likes to help. We always know the rules, so people trust us to judge contests. We tell the truth, and we don't take bribes."

What did she know about the Rose Kingdom?

"We like to grow things," the princess said, remembering her Royal Geography lessons. "If you visit our kingdom, your eyes will feel happy and rested after a day of looking at our velvety fields. You'll eat well, too, because we're good farmers."

Who was she kidding? As soon as people knew who she was, all of this imposter speech-giving was going to reflect badly on her family.

Ugh.

A pounding on the door put the princess in a panic about the egg. She covered it up, even though that wouldn't stop

A Library Crisis

Queen Ash, and unlocked the door.

To her great relief, Bridget came in with a giant pie.

"I didn't know I still got meals delivered."

"You don't," Bridget said. "So, how are the speeches coming?"

The princess was wary. "Okay, I think."

"Let's hear one."

The princess shrugged. It was like someone had poured cement in her mouth, and it had instantly set. Even with the rook egg in her hand, there was no possible way to make a sound.

"Maybe later?"

The princess nodded. She gave Bridget her sketch of the Tournament platform with escape hatch.

"That bad, *huh*?" Bridget cleared her throat. "The bad news is, you're going to have to practice without the egg."

Why take the egg away from the only person who could hatch it for her? Maybe the queen only wanted proof the egg hadn't hatched.

Or Queen Ash might be making a point that the princess couldn't keep anything from her. No need.

"The Golden Parsnip?" the princess finally managed the words.

"Yeah, sorry." Bridget held out her hand, and the princess put the egg in it. Even without the threat of the Golden Parsnip, they couldn't risk Queen Ash finding out about the secret room and the treasures of the PAL.

"If anyone can get it back, it's you." Bridget went out, leaving the princess to lock the door or not. "Give me a head start so the queen doesn't notice we're in cahoots."

A moment later, Bridget stuck her head back in. "If it

makes you feel better, I'll show your plans to the Dungeon Master. He'll get it built for you. Those monkey-bar handholds under the platform are sweet."

"It might come in handy, thanks," the princess said. A Plan B was a beautiful thing.

When her family came back, the dungeon staff was going to get so many Medals of Honor they'd have to build a display cupboard.

In the meantime, the princess had to convince Queen Ash to trust her with the egg until it hatched. The battle over the chick could come later.

The princess hid the PAL REFERENCE books under the bed covers and was about to follow Bridget and the egg, when she heard something.

Chirp!

The chick? But Bridget had just taken the egg, and the corridor was already empty.

Chirp! It was coming from inside the princess's cell . . .

She picked up the tray and put her ear to the pie.

Chirp!

It was a good thing the egg hadn't hatched. The chick would've been traumatized for life. Seriously.

Judging by the chirping, the princess was pretty sure the pie got baked first, and the birds went in afterwards.

She picked up the pie and looked underneath.

Bingo!

The bottom of the pan had a little round door.

She slid it carefully open, and a bird's foot popped out.

Well-trained, these pie messengers. The princess unfastened the message tube and pushed the scrabbling foot back inside. Gently, she set down the pie and opened

A Library Crisis

her message.

❧❧❧

To: Princess Melanie, Sibyl #7

   Dear <u>Whichever Cousin you are</u>,

   Terrible news: PAL librarian called to Fairy Godmother Court for copyright infringement.

   Waiting for critical part.

   Will leave as soon as possible.

   In friendship,

   Nero

   Crown Prince of the Blackfly Kingdom

   P.S. Sorry about the pie. All out of carrier pigeons.

   P.P.S. Counted 14 Cochem cousins. Did you remember your name yet? Nobody here seems to know it either.

❧❧❧

When the princess finally got outside, she heard shouting. A ring of protestors bearing signs marched in a circle in front of the Tower's entrance. Every color of the Seven Kingdoms was in this unexpected parade.

"A Li-brar-eeeee should be free!"

"We NEED to READ!"

"A Book for Every Nook!"

"Down with Fake Facts!"

And most worrisome of all:

"Why Does the Blackfly Prince have a PAL Library Card?"

"Library cards for everyone!"

Darnell Brummer and Hildy Nippes and the other back benchers were also there. As the princess passed through, one back bencher told another that Queen Ash was selling all the rare books from the PAL. Their signs read:

"Stop the Disappearing Books!"

"Books Shouldn't Vanish!"

Actually, the rare books were in the secret room in the dungeon, but the rumor needed squashing before Queen Ash got any ideas. Look at the way she'd jumped on the AirCastle thing. If she saw this protest, she'd hunt down the missing books and send them to Frankfurt. The princess had to make these protestors vanish as quickly as possible.

The Dungeon Master stood guard at the Tower's entrance, but the firefighters were slouched against the wall below, apparently enjoying the show. The Fire Chief should spend less time drinking tea with Cook and more time supervising his staff. If the Seven Kingdoms stormed the PAL in this mood, they would clean it out.

Hopefully, the promise of a library card would be enough to hold everyone until Hugh got back. He'd have apoplexy if the PAL books were checked out to readers all over the Seven Kingdoms. The princess heard his growl in her head: "*How will I get them back?*"

Coming up behind the firefighters, she checked her magical disguise and nudged the biggest firefighter there. "We need to go up and help the Dungeon Master, *uh*, secure the door."

The big firefighter looked down at her. "Who says?"

"*Uh*. Fire Chief's orders."

The firefighter's eyebrows lifted, but he shrugged. "Up to the Dungeon Master! Let's go, people!" He led the charge through the parade of picketers, with the princess and the other firefighters right behind.

A moment later, the princess was close enough to the Dungeon Master to tell him her plan. "If the firefighters can guard this door for a few moments, we can set up a table in

A Library Crisis

front of the PAL for library cards."

Unfortunately, the biggest firefighter overheard. "The Fire Chief gave you all those orders? I swear I've never seen you before."

The Dungeon Master faced him down. "The Fire Chief's plan is excellent. Please thank him from me personally."

He stepped in front of the princess, put his hand behind his back, and dropped his keys into her hands. She wasn't sure why he believed her, but she added it to her reasons for his Medal of Honor.

With the Dungeon Master between her and the crowd, the princess unlocked the Tower door and slipped through the smallest possible opening. At the top of the stairs and breathing hard, she unlocked the door marked broom closet and went in.

Looking around, the princess was impressed with what the Dungeon Master had accomplished. The PAL looked shabby, instead of disastrous, and the books she had spread out were dry to the touch. Buckets stood under the leaky places in the roof. Someone had swept the old wallpaper away. Moving down the tables at top speed, the princess clapped the books shut and stacked them in neat piles.

Thunk, thunk, thunk.

By the time the Dungeon Master came in, she was seated at a library table by the door with a stack of applications, a cup of fountain pens and a rubber stamp. It was the overdue stamp, but she hoped no one would notice. Hugh must have locked up the official PAL stamp or taken it with him.

"That looks perfect." The Dungeon Master drew up two chairs on the opposite side of the table so people could sit down to fill out their applications. "I should warn you. They're all talking about which books they want."

"*Uh, oh.*" The princess winced. She took a deep breath, glad that she didn't have to tell Hugh that. "We'll have to figure it out later. The important thing is to know who checked out what."

The Dungeon Master took the keys from the princess, locked Hugh's office, and the reference shelf. He smiled at her. "Let's keep it simple for now. You do the applications, and I'll check out the books."

Footsteps echoed on the stairs. The princess braced herself for the guests and hoped Queen Ash was too busy with Bridget and the egg to join the crowd.

The first person in the door wore a reassuringly yellow gown.

"Name and kingdom?" the princess asked.

"Princess Saffy, Saffron Kingdom."

The princess filled in the form and stamped it with the overdue stamp.

"Sign here, please. Next?"

Princess Saffy cleared her throat. "Can I check out a book about guinea pigs?"

The princess smiled at her. "Yes, checkouts are at that table. Just show your copy of the application form."

"Thanks, do all the PAL librarians wear yellow? It's very friendly." Princess Saffy already had her eye on the animal section. The princess whispered to the Dungeon Master. "Can you get a firefighter to stand on each side?"

It didn't make any more sense to be a firefighter working at the PAL, but at least she'd keep looking like the same person.

"One moment." The Dungeon Master stuck his head out the door, and two firefighters pushed their way to the princess's side.

Just in time. Darnell Brummer and Hildy Nippes were next. The princess spent a few extra minutes pointing out the section:

Damage to Library Materials

She made a big show of checking their signatures to make sure they signed their own names.

After that, a constant stream of people came in, got library cards, and went out with books. Everyone was cheerful but the princess who tensed whenever the door opened.

The Indigo crown prince gave orders to put their tent back up so they'd have a shady place to read.

Once everyone had a library card, the princess got lots of requests for help finding books. To keep from flickering like a rainbow, she took her firefighters along.

The Fire Chief drew her aside and whispered, "Have you got any love poems? You know, for cooks?"

Love poems wasn't really her area, but she showed him the poetry section and left him reading *When Sparks Fly*.

The princess didn't apply for her own library card, because she didn't want a fake. She wanted one with Hugh's official PAL stamp and her real name. As soon as he found out about today's work, he would ban her from the PAL for life.

When the Dungeon Master had locked up after the last new library patron, the princess put the broom closet sign back up again and jogged down the stairs to see a queen about an egg.

TROUBLE WITH PARSNIPS

As soon as she stepped out of the Tower, her dress turned black. She spun around to see who had triggered it, hoping for Nero, with her family close behind.

As Queen Ash and the Bishop came up to the princess, the queen said, "I've told you already. We're planning a Tournament, not a christening."

Oh, no.

"There you are," Queen Ash said. "Look, Bishop—a Blackfly princess from head to toe."

The princess made a small bow and stepped away from the queen, but it didn't help, because Queen Ash immediately closed the gap. The princess's gown stayed black.

"A princess has to be careful of her APPEARANCE." Queen Ash laid an arm over the princess's shoulders so she couldn't escape.

"Good evening," the Bishop said. "I don't think we've met. I received a message from a Cochem princess, but the whole family is away."

"It was me, I mean, I sent you a message," the princess said.

The Bishop looked stern. "I hope this isn't some kind of prank."

"My–" The princess didn't get a chance to explain about the croquet fever or her fairy godmother gift gone wrong.

"I'll make sure it won't happen again, Bishop." Queen Ash cut the princess off. "If we see a Cochem princess without a name, we'll send you a message."

The Bishop frowned at the fake Blackfly princess. "It's a shame to travel all this way for nothing."

"Don't–" the princess began.

A Library Crisis

"Have a good trip home!" Queen Ash produced a nauseatingly fake smile for the Bishop. He started down the path to the fast staircase towards Cochem. A bird flew overhead, and the Bishop stopped to admire it.

The princess's face got hot. She couldn't prove she was the Cochem princess he was looking for. She pretended this was a Pepper Pot at the Peppermint Tea House. *Say one thing.* "Ma'am, I need . . . my ROOK EGG."

"Nonsense." The queen patted her pocket. "It will be quite safe with me. I'm not as changeable as some people."

Ignoring the veiled warning, the princess took a deep breath and gave it one more try. "To practice my speech—my speeches—I need the ROOK EGG."

"Why would you need to practice? You're not supposed to . . ."

Win. That was what the queen meant, but the Bishop had come back up the path.

"Have you really got a rook egg?" he asked. "I've always wanted to see one."

The queen's mouth snapped shut. She pulled out the egg and set it, none too gently, in the princess's open palm. "I hope it bites you. Just don't forget I can get it back any time I want. And I will, if you fiddle with your name before the Tournament."

She swept off without a backward glance.

When she was out of earshot, the Bishop clapped his hands very softly and bowed his head to the princess. "There's a time to stand up to bullies."

Her Blackfly gown was gone, and she was wearing an acolyte's robe to match the Bishop. If he noticed, he didn't react.

TROUBLE WITH PARSNIPS

"Thank you." She couldn't look at him, but her whole face glowed with pleasure that she'd spoken up, and someone had heard. It wasn't so different from the triumphant night at the Speech or Die. "If you'd like a room at the Peppermint Tea House, King Oliver will pay for it."

The Bishop inclined his head. "I'll enjoy that, thank you."

"Excuse me, Bishop. I have to keep it safe until it hatches." She put the egg in her pocket and went off to put it under the brooder.

"I'm a birder," he called after her. "So I know about Cochem princesses. I don't know why I didn't recognize you before."

As the princess headed towards the dungeon, the glow of her tiny victory faded. Queen Ash still had the Golden Parsnip, and now she knew about the christening. The princess had to watch her step.

She worried about her parents. It would be like Queen Ash to lock them in the Blackfly dungeon accidentally-on-purpose until the Tournament was over.

🦢🦢🦢

In comparison with the day of the Library Crisis, the day before the Tournament was calm.

One young prince challenged another over who got to read Book Three of the *Seven Kingdoms Fairy Tale* series first, but the challenge turned into a hilarious water fight after the princess provided water balloons in seven colors.

A kerfuffle between the Magenta and Marigold Queens about who had inked the crossword puzzle in the latest issue of *Seven Kingdoms Magazine* settled into stilted politeness. Then the princess put out a cup of freshly-sharpened pencils with extra strong erasers, and the two queens started helping each other with the clues.

With the guests mollified and the Bishop accounted for, the princess was only missing her parents. If she'd had someone to talk to, the wait would have been easier.

After weeks of practicing her speech, Bridget found out about the fake Entry Forms, and that only Nero and the princess were allowed to speak. Bridget's silence was more biting than anything she could have said.

The princess was counting on her parents showing up before she had to actually . . . cheat.

CHAPTER NINETEEN

The InterKingdom Tournament

ON THE MORNING of the Tournament, someone pounded on the door of the princess's cell. She leapt for the REFERENCE books and stashed them under the bedcovers. The Tournament couldn't be starting already, could it? Her heart started to thump.

The window in the dungeon door banged opened from the outside. A dusty Blackfly prince peered through the grille. "Hello? Are you in there?"

"Nero!" The princess tried to see if her family was with him but he was blocking the whole window.

"You're sure you're a Cochem princess?" Nero snapped out.

"*Uh*, yeah." She was also sure they'd been over this.

"Then why aren't you challenging Queen Ash to a Pepper Pot Duel?" Nero yanked on the cell door. He must not like Queen Ash's crooked Tournament either. It opened, and he fell backward on the stone flags like a crab. "*Ow!* You aren't even locked in."

For a split second, the princess thought about locking

him out until he calmed down. She scouted the corridor, but her family wasn't there. After their long illnesses, King Oliver and Queen Sibyl had more pressing things to do than visit their youngest in the dungeon. "Are my parents up at the hall?"

Nero got to his feet and dusted his palms. His eyes never left her face. "Your parents?"

The princess wondered what was wrong with him. "King Oliver and Queen Sibyl."

"Wrong." Nero looked every inch a Crown Prince on the battlefield. "A Cochem princess would have already challenged Queen Ash."

The princess had already been over this with Bridget. Losing a Pepper Pot Duel to Queen Ash wouldn't solve the cheating. The situation called for King Oliver and Queen Sibyl—as soon as Nero got out of the princess's way. "It'd be much easier if you—"

"If I stood on a balancing board in our dungeon over the Rhine River for a few weeks?" Nero's face was white with fury. Had Queen Ash really threatened him with the Blackfly dungeon?

The princess wrinkled her nose. Nero must have forgotten that Queen Ash couldn't keep the Golden Parsnip once King Oliver arrived. Queen Ash wasn't in charge of the Tournament any more. Hunger must be clouding his thinking. He might have gotten lost a few times on the way and run out of rock-hard gingerbread.

"King Oliver will, *uh*, straighten out the Tournament. Why don't you, *uh*, come and get some parsnip fries?"

Nero took a deep breath. "King. Oliver. Isn't. Here. That's what I've been trying to tell you. You have to challenge

Queen Ash before this Tournament ties the Seven Kingdoms in knots."

Oh. King Oliver must still have a touch of fever. "Queen Sibyl could do it," the princess said.

"She's not here either," Nero said.

"A Harold or a Sibyl, then," the princess said with a touch of impatience. One of her siblings would work just as well for the Pepper Pot, but no parents meant no christening. She stared at the stone floor, trying to take it in.

Nero shook his head. "How long are you going to hide behind this I-don't-know-how-to-give-a-speech nonsense? No one is born knowing how to give a speech."

"Who cares?" The princess was done. Nero couldn't be bothered to remember her parents, but she was supposed to give a speech for him. "Give your own speech if you want one so bad."

"The Cochem honor is at stake, so a Cochem royal has to challenge." Nero's hands were on his hips.

"If you'd brought ANY of the SIXTEEN other people who could challenge Queen Ash to a Pepper Pot duel, it would be no problem." The princess's words flowed out as if she'd pulled a lever. "I don't see how I'm responsible for your mother. Why don't you tell her you won't do it?"

Oops. The deafening silence in the cell told the princess she'd said too much even while the words left her mouth. Speaking up for yourself was treacherous. Banging tools around was less likely to hurt people's feelings.

Nero's voice was like ice, and his bow wasn't any warmer. "Excuse me, I have to see Queen Ash about an Entry Form."

He went out, and the princess wished she'd locked him in while she'd had the chance. As soon as he pulled his Entry

The InterKingdom Tournament

Form, Queen Ash would cancel her crooked Tournament.

Without King Oliver and Queen Sibyl, everyone would go home.

The princess had bought a little time with the PAL library cards, but the books wouldn't keep the guests here if there was no Velvet Purse. They'd just take the books with them. Her parents' time was up.

Cochem was going to have the first invisible princess in the Seven Kingdoms. She put the rook egg in her pocket and went out of the dungeon to see the world before it couldn't see her.

But the castle grounds were full of people. Everyone but the Cochem royals were there.

From the portcullis to the front edge of the platform, two lines of Blackfly archers stood facing each other. Their black bows and arrows made them look like giant beetles. Queen Ash stood under the bristling arch.

A grim Nero stood at her side, so he must not have pulled his Entry Form. He'd told her once, "The queen commands, the prince is her foot soldier," but she hadn't really understood. Nero had been a friend, but the famous Blackfly temper had finally come to life. She rubbed away a sudden chest pain.

At the edge of the colorful crowd, the princess felt hollow. She had to get out of this crooked Tournament all by herself. Maybe she could steal her own Entry Forms. But one look at the Entry Basket surrounded by Blackfly archers killed that hope.

The queen took Nero's hand and raised it in the air as if he'd already won the Tournament. "Nero's here—what are we waiting for?"

"The Cochem family," the princess called out, surprising herself. Queen Ash couldn't start until every kingdom was present.

Nero shot her a funny look, seemed to catch himself, and went back to staring stonily into the distance.

"A technicality." Queen Ash clapped her hands, and the Blackfly archers formed a tunnel with their long black bows. "One member of the family is enough."

The guests nearest the queen murmured about not seeing any Cochem royals.

Queen Ash couldn't beat all Seven Kingdoms if the princess couldn't give the one losing speech she could give without cheating—her own. "No one can see who I am," she said, but the queen had moved on. The princess wasn't going to be able to stop her.

"Higher, you fools, you'll knock my crown off!" Queen Ash processed through the Blackfly archer tunnel and stopped at the front edge of the platform. "Welcome to the InterKingdom Speech Tournament! May the best speaker win the Velvet Purse." She held up the burgundy-velvet, oddly-lumpy, bag.

It must have rocks in it. Queen Ash had even spent the coins she'd found in Cochem Castle's seat cushions.

She leaned over the Entry Basket and pulled out the first Entry Form. Then the Blackfly archers surrounded the Entry Basket. No chance to take anything out.

Suddenly dizzy, the princess sat down on the grass and put her head between her knees. If the queen's next words were "Off with her head!" it would be a relief.

"The first speaker for the Saffron Kingdom will be ... Princess Mustardseed of Minnesota!" Queen Ash repeated the name very slowly and pointed to the small platform in front of the Saffron tent.

"Who's that?" someone called out.

"Never heard of that princess. Somebody get me the Royal Family Tree!"

The Royal Family Trees in the PAL were going to get a workout after the Tournament. Princess Mustardseed wasn't on any of them. The crowd clapped, but the princess was too dizzy to stand up.

Queen Ash repeated her announcement and the clapping started up again and faded away to confused chatter.

The princess pulled herself to her feet. She had to keep everyone here as long as possible, in case her parents still made it. As long as she was visible, there was still a chance. She could be speechless in front of the crowd, and that could be her first terrible speech. The thought of crossing the castle lawn to the Saffron tent seemed impossible. She sagged against the stone wall of the castle.

Then suddenly Bridget was there, pulling on her sleeve. "Come ON—we have to get you down there. I can't stand the whole thing, but I can't just let you blink out like a light."

The princess wasn't sure if Bridget was helping her or torturing her and couldn't ask. If she opened her mouth to ask or say thank you, she was going to be sick. Concentrating on her feet, she let Bridget pull her across the lawn behind the tents where no one was looking.

Bridget stopped behind the Saffron tent. "Go straight up and onto the platform before you look at anyone. Then take a deep breath first. It makes it easier."

Bridget sounded just like the Dungeon Master. The princess gave her a weak smile. Still focusing on her feet, the princess followed the edge of the tent to the platform ladder and climbed up to the platform, now in a yellow dress. The crowd burst into applause.

"Hey, you're that princess from the other day who helped us with the tent poles." The Saffron princess with the knitting took hold of her and dragged her to center stage. "You don't look so hot. Take a deep breath first."

Then the princess was standing in front of the Seven Kingdoms, flanked by Saffron royalty, and feeling like the only one there. The pennants on the tents whipped in the breeze, and little puffy clouds floated above the vineyards, but her family wasn't even in sight.

She reached into her pocket and touched the rook egg. The sea of people swatting blackflies in front of her almost knocked her down. They weren't smiling in the encouraging way people did at the VVL.

Of course they weren't. They wanted to hear people from their own kingdoms. People who had something to say and knew how to say it. People like Bridget who had practiced their speeches for weeks.

The princess took a step backward, and her yellow gown sprouted an apron. "I can't do this."

"Yes, you can." The certainty in Bridget's voice pushed the princess forward again, and the apron vanished. The crowd murmured. Queen Ash stood up and glowered at the princess.

"No." The princess was shaking uncontrollably now even though she was holding the egg in her pocket. "The Tournament is about everyone having their say. If I'm going to give a terrible speech, I want to do it for the right reasons."

The InterKingdom Tournament

Bridget gave her an appraising look. "I was wondering when you were going to catch on. The Dungeon Master said you wouldn't let us down."

Heat rose in the princess's face, and she climbed down from the Saffron platform.

"Now what?" someone called out.

"Princess Mustardseed of Minnesota!" Queen Ash shouted. "You're wanted on the Saffron platform."

"Let's do the Pepper Pot Duel," the princess said as soon as they reached the shelter of the tents. "I'll bring up the Speaker Meters while you issue the challenge."

Bridget grabbed her arm. "It has to be a member of the host family. That's why it's so rare. It's like objecting against your own family. I mean Queen Ash isn't part of your family, but she's hosting the Tournament in Cochem with the Golden Parsnip. So that means you."

"Yeah, but . . . " the princess said, but the point of the challenge was to win it, and she had no illusions about coming up with a winning speech. Terrible speeches were hard enough. "If I stand next to Queen Ash, I look like a Blackfly."

Bridget picked up the pace. "In a weird way, that might even help. Blackfly challenging Blackfly might be easier to explain. I thought you didn't want a crooked Tournament in Cochem. So do you, or don't you?"

"Okay," the princess said. They were at the Cochem platform. Deep inside, she'd already known she had to go through with it. She just hadn't expected the shaking to be so bad.

"If Queen Ash wins, things will get worse. Better start thinking about what will get a strong audience reaction."

Bridget went off to the dungeons at a run. "I'll have the Speaker Meters up in a jiffy."

The princess climbed up on the Cochem platform. Queen Ash kept trying to sweep VVLers out of her way, but they paid no attention. The Blackfly archers were trying to aim around Queen Ash but having a hard time because she wouldn't stand still.

The princess put her fingers in her mouth and whistled. The Fire Chief and the firefighters jogged around the corner of the castle, but the princess ignored them.

In the split second before anyone spoke, she shouted, "I-challenge-you-to-a-Duel-of-the-Pepper-Pot-because-of-fake-Entry-Forms," and sat down on the platform before she fell over.

CHAPTER TWENTY
The Pepper Pot Duel

THE FIRE CHIEF and fire fighters pushed through the crowd, looking for a fire to put out, but everyone's attention was on the Blackfly queen. Hidden in their midst, the princess sat on the gravel, stunned by what she had done.

"You challenge ME to a Pepper Pot?" A smile broke out on Queen Ash's face. "What a delightful surprise! I accept. You do realize you have to give the challenger's speech?"

Nero looked straight at the princess, and his look of respectful surprise was almost worth the terror that gripped her.

What had she done? Three sentences, she told herself, but a vision of ice-capped mountains rose up in her mind. She forced her teeth to stop chattering long enough to whistle.

The princess crawled closer to the fire fighters to adjust her disguise then pitched her voice low. "Let's clear that corner of the platform, ladies and gentlemen. We need to set up the Speaker Meters."

The Fire Chief looked a little perplexed, but the firefighters leapt into action. Speaker Meters were installed on the platform, and volunteers from three kingdoms

TROUBLE WITH PARSNIPS

volunteered to be Readers. The well-loved judge, King Pink, was among them.

Queen Ash flipped a coin. Her "Parsnips! I go first!" surprised nobody. She strode to the podium and smacked down the gavel. "People of the Seven Kingdoms, how dare you accuse my Tournament of crookedness! I will set loose plagues of blackflies in all your kingdoms."

"Noooo!" said the crowd, and the Speaker Meter dropped to minus 5.

The princess leaned over to Bridget. "I thought she needed a high score? What's she doing?"

Bridget said, "She needs the BIGGEST score—it can be highest or it can be lowest—it just can't be in the middle."

Wracking her brain for cheerfulness, the princess pictured éclairs floating merrily in the dessert sluice.

But Queen Ash's voice was too strong.

The water in the princess's imaginary sluice began to boil. Whipping cream wilted and chocolate icing ran. The water turned muddy brown, and clouds of steam filled the hall just like the day of the failed christening.

Queen Ash thundered at the crowd. "And since there are no parsnips, you will all be eating *Schwarzwurzel* to the end of your days."

"No, no! Not the dreaded black root!" someone called out.

"We want our parsnips!"

The princess groaned.

The Speaker Meter dropped to minus 7, but Queen Ash wasn't finished. "Here's my invitation to all the Crown Princes and Crown Princesses of the Seven Kingdoms. I have a little plan for hospitality in the Blackfly Kingdom dungeon. The one with the balancing board that lets you

The Pepper Pot Duel

swing back and forth above the water of the Rhine . . . until you get too tired to hold on."

The crowd moaned, and the Speaker Meter reading dropped lower. The end of the queen's speech met with stunned silence.

After a moment, King Pink stood and delivered the rating: "Minus 9 on the Scale."

Minus 10 was the lowest possible score. Disapproving murmurs swept through the audience. If the princess gave a happy speech, she'd have to get a rating of more than 10 to win. Impossible.

Wondering why she'd thought a duel would help, the princess stepped up to the podium to do her duty. Her idea wasn't very good, but it was all she had. She took a deep breath, cleared her throat, and called out as loud as she could, "The Palace Agricultural Library is closing in FIFTEEN minutes. Please bring your books to the checkout counter. Thank you for reading!"

The prince on the end of the front row clapped his graphic novel shut. "*Yippee!* Now I can get Book Four!" He disappeared down the hill, with the other graphic-novel fans right behind.

Everyone else in the Seven Kingdoms audience picked up their books and stampeded to the PAL.

The tiny silver ball of the Speaker Meter rose up so fast that it burst out the top of the Speaker Meter and sailed up into the air. A Cochem rook, seeing it glitter in the sun, swooped down, caught it and flew up to the top of the Tower.

"Out of Sight." King Pink read the Meter. "For a very, very —may I say it?—unusual speech."

Queen Ash shouted, "That wasn't a speech. It wasn't even a paragraph!"

A fierce "*Shhh!*" came from the sole remaining guest at the end of the front row. The tiny princess turned the page of her book and read on.

Nero and Bridget went flying after the library patrons, as extra support for the Dungeon Master. They had to check the books in and out and get the new Entry Forms filled in. The princess waited for the ruling.

On the platform, the judges counted on their fingers with furrowed brows. Queen Ash glowered at them. "Her speech was much too short. She should be disqualified. I am the REAL winner."

"The speech met the three sentence minimum." King Pink gave Queen Ash a stern look. "The Pepper Pot Duel Winner is hereby . . . " He looked over at the princess. "What's your name again, my dear?"

A tiny sigh escaped her. "Fifteenth."

"Oh, right, of course." King Pink seemed a bit flustered. "I had forgotten. The winner of the Pepper Pot Duel is Fifteenth. Now, if you'll excuse us, we also have a few books to return. Go ahead and straighten things out."

"Nooooooo!" Queen Ash pushed the princess out of the way and stood nose-to-nose with King Pink.

"The length of the speech doesn't matter, your Majesty," King Pink said, patiently. "It's whether the speech MOVES people. I really must be going, ma'am. I've got to get to the library before it closes."

"Thank you." No one heard the princess. She would rather dispose of the old Entry Forms without an audience anyway. If she'd already vanished, she could have done it

The Pepper Pot Duel

even with the Blackfly archers standing guard, but the price for that invisibility cloak was too high.

This called for Plan B. Quickly.

The princess wanted the Tournament to be running smoothly when her parents arrived. They had to get here soon, didn't they? If they didn't, they might never see her again.

She dragged the podium, with a terrible scraping sound, to the very center of the platform, but Queen Ash screeched so loud no one seemed to notice.

The princess came up behind the archers, checked her disguise, and asked, "Aren't we supposed to be lined up with that podium?"

Loudly blaming each other for not paying attention, the archers moved right where the princess wanted them. They set the Entry Basket in the center of their circle, right over the trap door.

Pleased with her work, the princess left them and took the tiny maintenance path around and under the platform to the moat.

She'd only been there a moment when Nero stuck his head under the platform.

"Nice Pepper Pot." His mouth quirked.

If he gave her a speech about how she should have done it, she was going to tackle him into the moat. "It worked."

Nero's lurking smile vanished, and he bent his head to her in a sort of half-bow. "It did. You saved me a few weeks hanging out on a board over the Rhine. I owe you." He hefted the stack of Entry Forms in his arms. "Where do you want these?"

"Uh. You can put them down on that rock where it's dry."

This was awkward.

Nero put them down. "Can I help?"

"Yes." The princess gave him the part she'd been looking forward to. She pointed to the monkey-bar handholds that led across to the trap door. "At the right moment, you can open the trap door. The Entry Basket should fall through, but a Blackfly archer or two might come with it. Will they follow your orders?"

Nero licked his lips. "Yep."

Then he was the right choice for the job. He swung across the monkey-bar handholds to the trap door and waited.

The princess checked the platform. The Blackfly archers looked clear. "Now!"

Nero yanked the string, the trap door opened. The Entry Basket fell into the moat with a splash and floated. The argument on the platform was still going on. Queen Ash seemed to be having it all by herself.

The princess hooked the floating Entry Basket with a lance she'd borrowed from the castle and pulled it over to shore.

Bridget, breathing hard from the hill, came up behind the princess with the final Entry Forms. "Sweet!"

"Can you shut that?" the princess called to Nero.

Nero pushed the trap door closed and leaned on the bolt, grunting. "It won't go in. One of those archers must have a foot on it."

Bridget shoved the papers towards the princess. "The one on top is yours. You have to sign it." Without waiting for an answer, Bridget swung over on the handholds to Nero.

The princess signed her own Entry Form and got the

The Pepper Pot Duel

same jolt all over again. Giving a Pepper Pot speech had been a once-in-a-lifetime stroke of luck.

This time, she had to give a speech that moved her royal parents to action in front of the Seven Kingdoms. A real speech.

This wasn't playing around with a hammer and saw and scraps of wood. This was using up expensive materials and making something that might not work. She felt quivery inside.

Bridget pushed the trap door up with both hands, and Nero put his shoulders to it. It went up another millimeter, but the bolt didn't budge. Normally, the princess was the one who did things like this, but this time she watched. People didn't know what they could do until they tried.

"Here," Bridget whipped out a tiny oil bottle and added a drop in the right place. The bolt slid home.

Bridget and Nero crossed back over the monkey bars and dropped down next to the princess.

The princess clapped. "That's twice in one day you got me unstuck."

Bridget dropped a curtsy. "Standard hospitality equipment."

"Handy to have around." Nero nodded approval.

The princess reached into the Entry Basket, started tearing up the strips of paper, and fed them to the fish.

"You printed Queen Ash's Entry Forms on rice paper?" Bridget asked.

"So the fish don't get sick," the princess said.

Nero and Bridget both looked at her. "You've been planning this the whole time, and you never mentioned it."

The princess shrugged. "Plan B."

TROUBLE WITH PARSNIPS

They were all ripping paper now. Nero found his own Entry Form and ripped it into tiny pieces. "Eat, eat!" he commanded the goldfish. The 500 goldfish did their duty.

"Okay, let's get this Tournament going again," the princess said. Nero laid the stack of new Entry Forms in the Entry Basket, and they carried it up onto the platform.

Queen Ash was shouting at her Blackfly archers who were hiding behind their black bows and arrows, looking miserable.

The princess looked at the trails in all directions. Her family had to arrive any moment, but there was no sign of them. "Is the Dungeon Master going to be able to close the PAL all by himself?"

"He was already locking up when we left," Bridget said. "Look, there are the first ones coming up the hill now."

A long, crooked, rainbow straggled up the hill from the PAL.

Perfect.

"Could you go, *um*, distract your mother?" the princess asked Nero.

"With pleasure." He went straight over to Queen Ash and bowed. His mouth moved, and Queen Ash slowly simmered down.

The princess went up behind the Blackfly archers again, set the Entry Basket down behind the nearest archer and tugged at his sleeve. "Aren't we supposed to be guarding that?" She pointed at the Entry Basket behind her.

"Oh, good call." He shouted at the others, "What happened to our formation here, people?"

"Re-group!"

The archers rearranged themselves around the Entry

The Pepper Pot Duel

Basket with the new Entry Forms. The Seven Kingdoms people were drifting back to the Tournament.

Check.

Then the princess glanced down at her hand and forgot everything else. She could feel her hand, but she couldn't see it. Her arm went next, and then she couldn't see any of the rest of herself, even when she turned all the way around.

She'd vanished.

NOOOO! No christening, no name, and out of sight for the rest of her life. She should be thankful she wasn't locked in the dungeon, but she wasn't. She wished she was in her workshop, right now, banging out the dents in her dessert sluice. Or banging new dents in.

As long as she could hit something.

Hard.

Then she looked up and felt even worse.

A familiar hot air balloon with silk panels in every color of the rainbow was landing on the lawn in front of the platform. The guests spread out in a big circle to make room.

The balloonists released more air, and the basket bumped gently on the ground.

The colorful silk slowly collapsed.

Four people climbed out of the basket, smiling and waving: Queen Sibyl, King Oliver, King Schwartz, and—unbelievable, but true—Harold number one.

They looked right through the princess.

So close.

And way, way too late.

They made Queen Ash look like Ms. Royal Punctuality.

Queen Ash was talking, and a rumble that might have been King Oliver answered her, but the princess only heard buzzing.

She had thought the christening was finally going to work out.

Tent poles.

Dishes.

Messages.

Bishop.

Pepper Pot.

Monkey-bar handholds.

Rice paper Entry Forms.

All for nothing.

She was more invisible than she'd ever been in her life.

CHAPTER TWENTY-ONE
Making a Name

KING OLIVER, QUEEN Sibyl, King Schwartz, and Prince Harold climbed up the stairs to the platform. The princess felt the weight of carrying a whole kingdom on her shoulders lift.

But then Prince Harold came towards her and she had to jump back at the last minute to keep him from stepping on her invisible feet. For a second, she'd forgotten her own personal nightmare.

"I guess you'll want this back now." With a ghastly smile, Queen Ash handed King Oliver the Golden Parsnip. Nero bowed his head, respectfully.

"Did you have a good time?" King Oliver attached it to his royal key ring. "Did you rule Cochem Fair and True?"

"There's no time for all that," Queen Ash said hastily, casting a quick glance at King Schwartz. "You've got a Tournament to run."

King Oliver and Queen Sibyl went to the podium together and drew an Entry Form out of the Entry Basket. Prince Harold went over to Nero. Even if they weren't old friends after all that croquet, they could see each other.

"Honored guests of the Seven Kingdoms." King Oliver's

voice boomed out. "Welcome to the InterKingdom Speech Tournament in Cochem!"

The crowd clapped politely, but without much enthusiasm. Maybe they were having a hard time believing in a Tournament by now. The whole front row was reading graphic novels.

"Is this a Do-Over?" someone called out.

"Our next speaker is Fifteenth of Cochem," Queen Sibyl read aloud.

Bridget hadn't mixed the Entry Forms. The princess's was still on top. Startled, she shot a look at Bridget who didn't react. *Of course.* Bridget couldn't see her either.

Queen Sibyl was still talking. "Oh, I can't wait to see her. She's the only one who didn't catch the fever." The crowd clapped again and fell silent as the king and queen moved to the side, waiting.

It was too late for a name now that she was invisible, but this was probably the last time anyone was going to ask the princess to say something. And she had some things to say.

Queen Sibyl stepped to the podium again, nearly brushing the princess off the platform. "Is Fifteenth here?"

The princess couldn't speak.

"Oh, Oliver, she must have gotten the fever after she sent us the balloon. I was sure she wasn't going to, and now she had it all alone. That's terrible!" Queen Sibyl hesitated on the edge of the podium, as if she couldn't quite see well enough to get down. She wiped her eyes with a silver handkerchief.

"She probably thought we forgot all about her. Poor, little thing!" King Oliver helped Queen Sibyl away from the podium. "You go and take care of her, Sibbie."

Making a Name

The princess reached out and touched Queen Sibyl's sleeve, but the queen didn't notice. How could she make her see?

Taking the rook egg out of her pocket, the princess set it on the podium and took her hand away. The egg appeared. "Mama, I'm right here."

King Oliver came to Queen Sibyl's other side. Both were staring at the egg in horror. "Oh, Sibbie."

The princess did matter to them. She began in a quavery voice. "Dear friends, family and honored guests—"

The crowd murmured.

"Who's speaking?"

"Never saw an egg give a speech before."

"Me neither."

"It can't be the egg. It hasn't even hatched yet."

"That's not fair!"

"Shush! I want to hear what it says."

The princess swallowed and fixed her gaze on the rook egg. When no one was listening, a speech was even harder. She called her parents by name since they couldn't know she was looking at them. "King Oliver, sir, and Queen Sibyl, ma'am—"

They kept looking past her and then back at the egg. The princess interrupted her speech. "I'm . . . okay . . . I didn't turn into an egg. I'm just invisible."

King Oliver gave a low moan. Queen Sibyl took in a quick, horrified breath, then pulled herself together. "That's okay, then, isn't it, Oliver." She took his hand, but tears ran down her face, unchecked. "Don't stop, Fifteenth, we're listening."

The princess went back to her speech before she lost her voice. "The Dungeon Master and his daughter, Bridget—"

Bridget made a startled sound, but the princess went on, "have made Cochem Castle welcoming to guests from the top of the Tower to the bottom of the dungeon. I would like to recommend them to you for the Medal of Honor."

"Hear, hear!" The crowd whistled and cheered, throwing the princess off her rhythm.

"*Brava!*" Nero shouted. "Well done!"

"Hip, hip, hooray!" The Indigo prince started a wave of cheers.

"An excellent idea!" Queen Sibyl and King Oliver clapped too. The princess couldn't take it in. They had heard her. A crooked smile spread across her face, and she couldn't stop it. This was an unbelievable feeling. She wanted to say all the biggest, best things she could think of.

She held up her hand and immediately took it down. It was hard to remember. One more thing had to be arranged before Hugh got back. "The people of the Seven Kingdoms have been issued temporary library cards. If we had a hot air balloon bookmobile, they could check out books and return them, no matter where they live."

The Seven Kingdoms went wild. The front row tossed their graphic novels in the air and caught them again.

King Oliver's whisper boomed out, "That would be charming, wouldn't it, Sibbie?" Carefully reaching for the mallet and laying a huge protective hand on the rook egg, he struck the podium. "Quiet, please, I'm sure we all want to hear what else Fifteenth has to say."

His slow movements had given her lots of time to move her invisible hands out of range. The last time he'd called for attention for her like that was at the christening. She cleared her throat to ask for the impossible. "Most of you know, the Duel of the Halls ended the christening party."

The princess looked out at the huge crowd of guests stretching across the lawn, and her mind blanked. She gripped the podium with both hands, feeling her face get hot. No one could see her turning red. She had to say something so they would know she was still here. "You can't see me ... because I didn't get a name in time, so my fairy godmother gift malfunctioned."

The princess didn't even hear any breathing on the platform.

"I'd still like a name." She forced the words out, shaking from the effort. Asking for yourself was much harder.

"We're AWARE," Queen Ash said, in a bored tone. "All this drama and you'll still end up Sibyl #8. Your parents have no imagination."

"Ash." Her royal husband handed Queen Ash a piece of black salt-water taffy and she subsided.

King Oliver choked. "With the fever and everything, we forgot about her name—again. Next year I'm getting my shot twice."

Queen Sibyl patted his hand. "Me, too."

The princess's voice shook. "The Seven Kingdoms are here. The Bishop is here. My parents are here. That's everyone we need. Could I have the name Twyla please?"

"What's that?" King Oliver patted his pockets as if he was looking for something.

"I didn't quite catch it," Queen Sibyl said in a halting voice. "Could you tell us again please, Fifteenth?"

Oh no. She had to say it all again. The princess closed her eyes and saw Mr. Giant and the Dungeon Master at the Speech or Die night. Say one thing. Give them the beginning, middle, and end. Loud and clear. She flung her words at the crowd. "The name is Twyla. It's spelled T-W-Y-L-A. Twyla."

She gave a tiny bow, forgetting her visibility issues again, but she couldn't let go of the podium. A long silence reminded her that they couldn't SEE she was finished. That stung.

Into the vast silence came a soft, cheeping sound and a distinct crack.

The egg!

Shell chips flew into the air, the cracks widened, and a small black head emerged. It opened its beak wide, directly at the princess. Her heart leapt. She was invisible, but the rook chick still knew where she was.

A black shape swooped down, and Queen Ash snatched the chick up from the podium. "It's MINE. Invisible princesses can't keep rook chicks. And I need it to eat those . . ." Her voice dropped to a whisper, "blackflies."

"No!" The princess was not giving up a Cochem rook chick to Queen Ash. She reached for it but by some instinct, Queen Ash held the chick high over the princess's head.

"*Caw, caw, caw!*" the rook chick cried.

King Schwartz brushed past the princess, excusing himself to the air, and came straight over to Queen Ash. "What have you got there, sweetheart?"

"It's MY rook." Queen Ash's lip stuck out. "Because now I won't win the Velvet Purse. I'll never get rid of those pesky THINGS unless this chick will eat them for me. I HAVE to have it. Isn't it sweet?" She crooned at the chick.

"*Callllll,*" it said and nipped at her fingers.

"It bit me! Nasty bird." Queen Ash dropped the chick onto

Making a Name

the podium and stuck her hurt fingers in her mouth.

The princess scooped it up, and the rook chick fluttered for balance in her hands. "There, there. I've got you."

"*Callllypso!*" the rook said. "Calypso."

The princess set the rook chick on the podium and took her hands away to show the crowd, still keeping her arms protectively around it. No one could see her arms, but they would feel them if they tried anything. "Thank you for coming to the Speech Tournament."

"NOOOO! Schwartz, get it back for me. I NEED it." Queen Ash's fingers were still in her mouth, but she stepped on King Schwartz's shoe with her spiky black one.

King Schwartz yelped. "Ash! You don't have to do that."

"The Blackfly Queen is kindly requested to sit down!" King Oliver's voice thundered across the Mosel valley. He strode over to Queen Ash. "You have caused nothing but trouble during this whole christening party. I only gave you the Golden Parsnip because Fifteenth seemed to want you to have it. But from what I hear, you didn't rule Cochem fair and true at all. She would have made a much better Regent. If you don't want to spend the rest of the party in the dungeon, you'd better be quiet."

A shocked silence fell over the Seven Kingdoms.

The princess's mouth dropped open. She'd never thought King Oliver would tell his sister to behave, no matter how outrageous she was. And he'd done it for the princess.

Ignoring them all, King Oliver gave his attention back to the podium where the invisible princess had finished her speech. He started to clap, and all Seven Kingdoms burst into applause.

His voice boomed out again, "Sibbie, do you like Twyla? It

has your YL."

"Very elegant." Queen Sibyl smiled. She stretched her arms out around the podium and brought them carefully together. The princess was squeezed tight in a royal hug. "Have I got you now, Fifteenth? You must have had a rough time here all by yourself. We got the fever right when you needed us. You had already been so patient with us for so long. I'm so proud of you."

"*Mmhh.*" The princess's eyes smarted. Queen Sibyl had found her even though she was invisible. The princess pressed her face against Queen Sibyl's arm.

"I like Twyla. It's special, just like you." Queen Sibyl stroked the princess's invisible hair. "You know, you never did like the front of the room. And you do so many marvelous things in the back. Look at your wonderful hot air balloon."

She'd seen her.

All this time.

The princess squeezed Queen Sibyl back. "Did you like it?"

"I did. Will you take me up again?"

Shy, careful Queen Sibyl liked the hot air balloon enough to go up in it again. The princess looked up to make sure. Queen Sibyl smiled down in the princess's approximate direction.

"You'd go up again too, wouldn't you, Oliver?"

"That balloon's even more exciting than croquet. The things you make in your dungeon workshop make me so proud. Your exploding confetti croquet mallet . . ." King Oliver wiped his eyes with his sleeve and couldn't go on.

"Really?" The princess smiled so hard it hurt.

Making a Name

Queen Sibyl's lip trembled in sympathy. "I thought you might not want to be a Sibyl but I should have asked you. I didn't want to put you on the spot. But tell me one thing—are you sure you want Twyla? You could have Amaryllis, like the beautiful red flowers that look like a speaking trumpet, or Merylin. It's kind of magical and pretty and means blackbird."

More names for her.

And none of them were Sibyl.

The princess blinked very hard, twice.

"But she chose Twyla," King Oliver struck in.

The princess's mouth fell open. King Oliver had been paying attention.

He added, "It means woven with a double thread, you know. There's a hidden side and a public side."

"I didn't know you knew that, Oliver." Queen Sibyl gave him an admiring look.

King Oliver put his arm around his wife, who still held the princess. "I wrote it down so I wouldn't forget. I wanted her to have a good name."

The princess dug into her pocket and pulled out the slip of paper she'd found on the rushes during the christening and laid it on the podium. "Papa, is this yours?"

King Oliver put his glasses on and carefully took the princess's invisible hand, turning the note so he could read it. "Look at that—I thought I lost it!"

The princess marveled. King Oliver had been thinking about her, all this time.

"No matter what name you choose, we love you." Queen Sibyl's voice broke.

King Oliver patted Sibyl's hand on his arm. "Good girl,

Sibbie, that's just what I wanted to say. Now, let's get on with the christening!"

The princess needed everyone on the platform. She set the rook chick down on the podium, cupped her hands around her mouth, and shouted.

"Keziah Akosombo!"

"She learned that from me," Queen Ash remarked to no one in particular.

Kizzy landed on the podium and squinted her eyes at the spot where the princess was standing. "Say something else so I can see where you are."

"Here," the princess said, picking up the chick again.

"Excuse me," Queen Sibyl's voice trembled, but she looked determined. "Fairy godmothers need to wait until after the christening. We don't want any gifts given too early. No offense, Kizzy."

"It's a little late for that, Mama." The princess touched Queen Sibyl's hand with one finger.

"Oh!" Queen Sibyl jumped, and then put her other hand over the princess's invisible one, around the rook chick. It made no attempt to bite Queen Sibyl.

"I'm really, really sorry about this—" Kizzy shook her head. At that moment, Hugh Ancry heaved himself up the stairs onto the platform, puffing hard.

"How did you get here?" the princess asked. He was supposed to be in Fairy Court.

Hugh looked over his shoulder and turned in a complete circle. At least he didn't look up in the air.

"Over here," the princess said and then when he looked past her again, "It doesn't matter where I am."

"Oh. Oh, I'm sorry. The hot air balloon didn't get here in

time then." Hugh's voice was gentler than she'd ever heard it. His eyes were shiny, and he actually sniffed.

"Thanks anyway." The princess didn't want to talk about it. "What happened to you?"

"I was charged with having an illegal-copy-of-a-fairy-reference-document." Hugh turned bright pink.

King Oliver grunted. "Unfortunate."

The princess had never seen Hugh like this. "Oh. Uh, sorry. I meant, how'd you get here so fast?" The Fairy Court was famous for its long trials. Fairies lived forever so they had a lot more time.

"I paid the fine." Hugh went back to his normal color. "They threw in the Fairy Godmother Transport after I pointed out that the PAL was a Seven Kingdoms Reference Collection. I should have used it to get your parents to you on time. I didn't think of it soon enough. But what about you? Can I do anything to help?"

Kizzy coughed. "Over and done with. Let her speak already."

Hugh turned pink all over again.

The princess wondered fleetingly if Kizzy had been reprimanded for that odd yellow stain in her book. But that was more than enough embarrassing questions. It was a relief to have Hugh back in one piece.

The Bishop wore his formal robes with a mitre on his head and a staff in his hand. He came over to the podium, very carefully leaving space. The princess felt like a china tea cup.

King Oliver pounded the podium with the gavel. "Let there be no further delay!" he ordered, in his grandest manner.

TROUBLE WITH PARSNIPS

In his quietest booming whisper, he added, "I liked that croquet mallet with the exploding confetti much better."

Laughter spread through the crowd. But at the word "croquet", a shudder passed through the princess and she studied her parents for signs of fever.

But King Oliver went right on, as if croquet no longer had the power to make him forget her. "Do you think you could make one of these with exploding confetti for the next Speech Tournament?"

The princess's heart gave a little skip. He had recognized her work even in the middle of a bout of croquet fever. "Yes, sir."

"Excellent," King Oliver said.

"Water." The princess could barely speak. Nero brought a clean glass over from the table where Queen Ash and the Bishop had been sitting and offered it to the air next to the rook chick. He looked worried and sorry, even though none of this was his fault.

The princess gurgled. "Not to drink! For the christening." She stuck her fingers in her mouth and gave the shrill whistle that summoned the firefighters.

Everyone covered their ears and stepped back from the platform.

"Can I borrow your handkerchief?" the princess asked. Nero handed it over and the princess wrapped the chick up in it and held it behind her.

The firefighters came running and set up the water pumps, aiming them at the platform. Queen Ash took one look and dragged King Schwartz off the platform. "Enough is enough. Let's go find the refreshments before they run out again."

The Bishop said the words of the royal baptism. "By the power invested in me, you are hereby baptized Princess Twyla of Cochem!"

Queen Sibyl blotted her eyes. King Oliver mopped his royal nose and gave the signal.

"Ready, Aim, WATER!" the Fire Chief bellowed.

Princess Twyla braced herself. A blast of cold water swept over her. She shrieked and the crowd laughed and broke into applause again.

The Fire Chief drenched the princess, and, for good measure, King Oliver, Queen Sibyl, Nero, Bridget, the Bishop, and the entire front of the castle.

"People of the Seven Kingdoms! I present to you the Fifteenth Child of Cochem, Princess Twyla." King Oliver held out his dripping hand.

Princess Twyla laid hers in it.

A few people in the crowd gasped.

"Are all Cochem christenings so WET?" someone asked.

"That's a very thoroughly christened princess."

King Oliver held up her hand, as if everyone could see her. And then Princess Twyla realized they could.

She was wearing her own white christening dress, white slippers, and a white princess hat, just like the Cochem princess she was. The only thing that was black was Nero's handkerchief, and the rook chick in it. What a thrill to be herself again!

"Hip, hip, hooray!" shouted Princess Saffy. The other kingdoms joined in with a roar of sound.

"Hip, hip, hooray!"

"Long live Princess Twyla!" Nero shouted behind her. He whipped the water from his black hair, but his bright smile said he didn't mind. "Nice to see you in your true colors at last. Brought you a present. That's what took so long."

He gestured to a huge crate the stonemasons had lowered next to the platform, and handed her a crowbar. "Have at it."

Princess Twyla cracked the wooden crate open with the crowbar and looked inside. A huge coil of industrial cable.

"You said something about building a cable ferry—" Nero rubbed the back of his neck and looked at her anxiously.

This was a whole different kind of speech giving. Say one thing. "It's the nicest present I ever got."

"Sorry I kept saying you had a head injury." Nero looked down and coughed. "I don't always see what I'm looking at, even if it's right in front of me."

Princess Twyla shrugged. "Industrial cable looks like perfect eyesight to me." She shot him a sideways smile. "Want to help?"

His face lit up. "I was hoping you'd say that."

EPILOGUE

Now that King Oliver and Queen Sibyl were back in Cochem, the InterKingdom Speech Tournament went on for another week. The rest of the Harolds and Sibyls showed up the next day and joined the audience. They'd been too busy playing croquet to write speeches or send in Entry Forms.

Princess Twyla was so glad to see them all that she almost missed their trails of colored index cards from the last Tournament. She looped contentedly from her workshop, where she was working on a dishwashing machine for Bridget, to the cable ferry construction site, to the Tournament, where she listened to speeches until her full head drove her back to her workshop.

She took a front row seat for the last two speeches of the Tournament, Nero's "The History of the Seven Kingdoms" and Bridget's "Speaking Clearly with Tact Is an Art."

Nero's speech was showy and brilliant and impressive and the applause was very polite afterwards. Nero gave a gracious bow and sat down next to Princess Twyla to listen to Bridget.

TROUBLE WITH PARSNIPS

"Anyone can make themselves heard when they have been granted a position of power," Bridget began, glancing at Prince Nero.

Everyone else looked at Queen Ash, but King Schwartz was keeping her very busy with saltwater taffy, so she didn't even stick out her tongue.

"But less powerful speakers have a choice too. I can close myself up like a tower." Bridget pointed up at Cochem's Tower and wrapped her arms around herself.

"What if you laugh at my speech? Or misunderstand my words? It might feel safer to defend myself against everything I think you might be thinking."

The crowd was silent. Princess Twyla remembered the painful moments on the Saffron platform.

Bridget went on, "But then you'll never hear what I want you to know. A clear speech takes a risk." She opened up her arms to the Seven Kingdoms guests.

"If I say one thing at a time, I help you follow. That's my magic as a speaker. Once I've said my one thing, you can love it or hate it, ignore it or let it change you. That's your magic as a listener. You have the power to change me too, because when you listen, you change the way I hear my own words."

The whole Seven Kingdoms jumped up from their seats, stomped their feet, threw flowers at the platform, and shouted.

"Bravo!" Princess Twyla shouted. She clapped her hands raw, and smiled so hard her face promised to hurt the next day.

Nero stood up and whistled. "Tell'em Bridget!"

Wrinkling his forehead, King Oliver looked at the Velvet

Epilogue

Purse, pulled out a rock, and emptied the Purse into the moat. He ordered it properly re-filled from the Cochem Treasury and gave Queen Ash a hard look across the podium that promised a reckoning. "Fair and True, Ash?"

Queen Ash turned her face away. King Schwartz covered his eyes with his hand. Twyla hoped Nero hadn't noticed.

King Oliver and Queen Sibyl conferred with the official judges, headed up by King Pink, and called Bridget back up to the podium.

Bridget blew kisses to the Dungeon Master and waved at Twyla, Nero, and the VVLers.

"How many ribbons you got now?" a back bencher called, but Bridget only smiled.

Cook waved a dishtowel, and catcalls from the back benchers only died down when the Fire Chief threatened them with the water pump.

"Congratulations!" Queen Sibyl said and handed Bridget the re-filled Velvet Purse. Bridget curtsied.

"And thank you for your loyalty to Cochem Kingdom." King Oliver shook her hand. "We are in your debt."

"Thank you, sir." Bridget curtsied again.

King Oliver started the clapping, and the crowd went crazy all over again.

After the excitement died down, Twyla took Bridget and Nero down to the workshop to show off the dishwashing machine.

※※※

The morning after the Tournament, after everyone but the Blackfly guests had left, Princess Twyla came into the hall, holding her rook chick in one hand and a small box in the other. King Schwartz and Queen Ash were leaving this

250

morning.

In the far corner, the queen shrieked, "How many times do I have to tell you? I can't eat raspberry tarts like this!" Bandages covered her hands and her cloud of blackflies was thicker than ever. "Or with these, terrible . . . THINGS." She waved her hands at the blackflies.

King Schwartz had his arm around her. "There, there, Ash."

Princess Twyla made her way over to them.

"Take that beast away!" Queen Ash pointed a shaking finger at the chick.

Twyla handed Queen Ash a small, gift-wrapped box with a huge, black-velvet bow. "I wanted to thank you for helping me get my name."

"For ME?" Queen Ash looked at her husband and ripped into the paper. Nestled inside soft cotton was an emerald green atomizer. "Perfume!" The queen lifted it reverently out of the box and misted herself. Blackflies fled from her in a cloud.

The rook chick snapped them up as they flew past.

Queen Ash looked startled.

"It's, *uh*, peppermint repellent." Twyla took a step back. "I found the recipe in the PAL."

"Schwartz," commanded the queen, spinning away from Twyla. "We're going home. We need to build a library. At once. A BETTER one than Cochem's with fashion magazines and all the newspapers that have me in them."

"The Balloon Bookmobile is leaving in fifteen minutes," Twyla said, and then cruised the head table for some snacks to take down to the workshop.

Nero was staying over for a while, to help with the cable

Epilogue

ferry. Twyla didn't mind. She couldn't wait to see the ferry in action and Nero's help would make it all go faster. He wouldn't fall into the moat or drift off into daydreams. A Crown Prince like Nero didn't sidetrack that easily.

☙❧☙❧

Thanks for Reading!

If you enjoyed TROUBLE WITH PARSNIPS, would you consider leaving a comment at your favorite online store? A word or two makes all the difference. You can also help other readers find this story by recommending it to your local library (in print or as an ebook on Overdrive).

THANK YOU SOOOO MUCH!

Laurel Decher

WANT TO SIGN UP FOR MORE STORIES?

If you like stories like this one, sign up for my Reader's List at https://LaurelDecher.com. If it's not your thing, unsubscribe at any time. About once a month, you'll get:

- my favorite book tips for your hungry readers,
- a round-up of my best blog posts,
- the inside scoop on my upcoming books.

Please Note: Minors must use a parent or guardian's email account. They may use their own only if a parent or guardian has access to it. (Please remind your kids that they should never communicate with an adult, even an author who has visited their school, without your knowledge and supervision!).

As a thank you, you'll get my most recent **Book Menu for Hungry Readers (9-12 years old)**. More great books to get from your local library or bookstore!

Join my Reader's List at https://LaurelDecher.com

Author's Note

Photo: © Jan Decher, 2018.

LAUREL DECHER writes stories about all things Italian, vegetable, or musical. Beloved pets of the past include "Stretchy the Leech" and a guinea pig that unexpectedly produced twins. She's famous for getting lost, but carries maps because people always ask her for directions.

HOW THIS STORY GOT STARTED: In school, I was the girl who didn't sharpen her pencil because she didn't like going up in front of the classroom. *The pencil sharpener is too noisy!* Everyone will look at me.

For years, I didn't know what my teachers looked like, but I can still see the floors. Tile is what you notice when you look down all the time. **TROUBLE WITH PARSNIPS** is about a much braver and more inventive person, the kind of person who looks up and sees everyone. The kind I want to learn to be.

As a grown-up, I went to a club called Toastmasters that teaches people how to speak up in the right way at the right time. It's kind of like Girl or Boy Scouts because you can earn "badges" for learning how to stand up in front of others. :)

The Vintner's Ventriloquism League in this story is a

Author's Note

wacky sort of Toastmasters club. If you haven't read the whole story yet, you don't meet them until Chapter 11. Toastmasters do a thing called "Table Topics" that is like the "Pepper Pot" in this story.

When I went to Toastmasters, I was a Girl Scout Leader, so our troop tried everything out at our meetings. Nobody looked at the floor. After a while, the girls ran the whole meeting. The leaders only got a few minutes to talk if they needed to announce something. It was cool.

So I started writing about a princess who didn't think she could ever give a speech.

Acknowledgements

Many thanks to Susan Graham, writer, editor, and mentor extraordinaire, who gave me the idea of communicating mixed signals to people when we try to foresee and answer all of their objections before they say them out loud. Broadcasting on more than one station makes static, not music.

Heartfelt thanks to my critique partners and all those who gave such excellent feedback and inspiration while I was working on this story. It's a privilege to know so many amazing authors!

Eileen Schnabel, author of *One if By Land, Two if By Submarine (Saving America Series #1)* read and re-read scenes and chapters with amazing patience and cheerfulness. Thanks SO much!!

Special thanks for help with this project to Kristi Wientge, author of *Karma Khullar's Mustache*, Halli Gomez, contributing author to *Brave New Girls: Tales of Heroines Who Hack (Brave New Girls #3)*, Richelle Morgan, master of copy that sings, Mark Holtzen, author of *A Ticket to the Pennant: A Tale of Baseball in Seattle*, Michelle Leonard, contributing author to *Brave New Girls: Stories of Girls Who Science and Scheme (Brave New Girls #2)*, Gabrielle K. Byrne, author of *Rise of the Dragon Moon*, Karin Lefranc, author of *I Want To Eat Your Books*, Olivia Kiernan, author of *Too Close to Breathe (Frankie Sheehan #1)*, Julie Artz, whizbang structure detector, and Sussu Leclerc, author of *Creating Unique Storyworlds: Essential tips and techniques for fiction writers (Writing tools Book 1)*. Many thanks to all the other talented members of The Winged Pen for their support: Rebecca Smith-Allen, Jessica Vitalis, Rebecca Petruck (*Boy Bites Bug*), Marty Mayberry, Gita Panjabi Trelease (*Enchanteé*), Kate Manning, Hilary Harwell, Jessica Vitalis, and Jennifer Park (*The Shadows We Know By Heart*)!

Thanks to Wade Albert White, author of *The Adventurer's Guide to Successful Escapes (Saint Lupin's Quest Academy* for *Consistently Dangerous and Absolutely Terrifying Adventures #1*), who gave early feedback on the synopsis and draft. Also to Kristine C. Asselin, author of *Any Way You Slice It*, and Jane Warren, who can solve a plot problem on the way to lunch.

Many thanks to Isabelle Decher, patient reader of drafts and author of the prize-winning short story, „Am höchsten Punkt ist die Geschwindigkeit null *[At the highest point, velocity is zero.]*" Thanks to Sophie Decher for working coffees and moral support of all kinds!

A grateful bow to Susan Gilbert-Collins, author of *Starting From Scratch*, insightful reader, and accountability partner for so many areas of my life!

Thanks to all my amazing speaker friends at Toastmasters of Greater Burlington, Vermont who showed me that speaking is something anyone can learn. I'm in awe of what you come up with!

Many thanks to Deborah Halverson for her Dear Editor contest during Revision Week and her insightful and encouraging comments!

To my valiant Girl Scout co-leader Becky Holt, our steadfast cookie chair, Dasha Zentrichova, and all the members of Girl Scout Troop #30402 who tried out Toastmasters Lite in our meetings! So proud of you all!

Patti Buff, Regional Advisor for the Germany + Austria Chapter of the Society of Children's Book Writers and Illustrators, thanks so much for all you make possible!

To Jane Park, my partner-in-writing and the expat life, and editor of *Germany for Beginners: The German Way Expat Guidebook*.